50일 롤플레잉 연습으로 실전 영어 끝내기

English for Everyday Activities

Karl Nordvall

Contributing Editor: Helen Kym

일상회화 **서바이벌편**

How to Use

- 영어권 국가에서 살거나 여행을 할 때 가장 많이 접할 수 있는 **10가지 Section, 50가지 상황** 학습
- 만화 속 캐릭터들을 통한 간접 체험, 상황에 딱 맞는 표현 익히기
- 상황의 흐름을 생동감 있게 **그림을 통해 전개**
- 영어권 국가에서 가장 많이 쓰이는 기초 **패턴 드릴**
- 스피킹의 퀄리티를 높이는 **롤플레잉** 활동

SECTIONS

영어권 국가에서 마주할 가능성이 높은 상황을 10개의 Section으로 정리하였습니다.

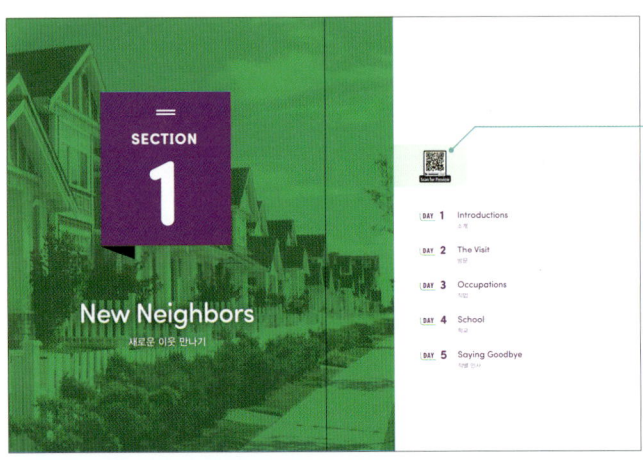

- 인강 QR을 스캔하여 각 DAY별 인강을 미리 보세요!
  전체 인강은 Talkit 앱에서 교재 시리얼 코드 입력 후 확인 가능합니다.

- **Talkit**: 스피킹 트레이닝 앱을 활용하여 다양한 스피킹 연습 가능

DAILY LESSONS

총 50일 학습 구성이며, Talkit 앱과 별도 판매되는 Activity Book을 통해 복습까지 함께 할 수 있습니다.

- Activity Book (별도 판매)

KEY VOCABULARY
각 Day별 중요한 단어, 표현 등을 실었습니다. 내가 모르는 단어나 표현을 먼저 익혀보세요.

KEY EXPRESSIONS
일상생활과 여행에서 만날 수 있는 상황에 맞는 패턴 드릴을 통해 언제 어디서든 원하는 말을 해보세요.

STUDY TIP
각 Day에서 추가로 배우면 좋을 문장 또는, 알아두면 좋을 문화 관련 포인트나 문법 어휘 포인트를 함께 제시했습니다.

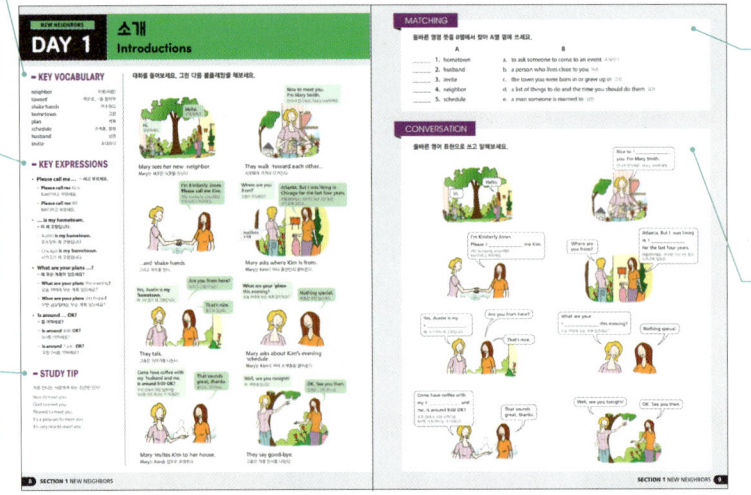

MATCHING
학습한 단어 및 표현을 Matching 활동을 통해 복습해보세요.

CONVERSATION
우리말을 보면서 학습한 영어 문장을 영어 표현으로 쓰고 다시 한번 말해보세요.

EEA: 일상회화 서바이벌편
5 STEP 학.습.법

1. **Lecture & Intro:**
EEA 인강 학습하기 & 음원 듣기

하루 10분 강의와 전체 음원을 들어보세요.

2. **Word Flash:**
주요 어휘 익히기

일상생활에서 자주 쓰이는 주요 어휘를 익히세요.

3. **Shadowing:** 오늘 학습한 표현이
입에서 술술 나올 때까지 여러 번 낭독하기

영어 문장을 5번씩 큰 소리로 읽어보세요.
입에 잘 붙지 않는 어려운 문장은 10번씩!

4. **Gap Fill:**
그림을 보고 빈칸 채우기

그림을 보고 영어 문장을 유추해 말해보세요.
영작이 되지 않는 문장은 다시 반복!

5. **Role-Playing:**
스피킹의 퀄리티를 높이는 롤플레잉

오늘 배운 표현을 원어민과 실제로 대화하듯 롤플레잉을 해보세요.
어느 순간 영어 스피킹이 자연스러워집니다.

스피킹 트레이닝 앱인 **Talkit**을 통해 **EEA: 일상회화 서바이벌편**의 **5 STEP**으로 학습해보세요.

Contents

SECTION 1 — New Neighbors
- DAY 1 — Introductions — 8
- DAY 2 — The Visit — 10
- DAY 3 — Occupations — 12
- DAY 4 — School — 14
- DAY 5 — Saying Goodbye — 16

SECTION 2 — Shopping
- DAY 6 — Women's Clothing — 20
- DAY 7 — Sizes and Trying Things On — 22
- DAY 8 — Men's Clothing — 24
- DAY 9 — Paying at the Counter — 26
- DAY 10 — Electronics — 28

SECTION 3 — Social Time
- DAY 11 — At a Fast Food Restaurant — 32
- DAY 12 — At the Movies — 34
- DAY 13 — Helping a Neighbor — 36
- DAY 14 — At a Coffee Shop — 38
- DAY 15 — At the Museum — 40

SECTION 4 — Around the Town
- DAY 16 — Taking a Taxi — 44
- DAY 17 — In the Library — 46
- DAY 18 — Taking a Bus — 48
- DAY 19 — Getting Gas — 50
- DAY 20 — Asking for Directions — 52

SECTION 5 — Restaurant
- DAY 21 — Arriving at the Restaurant — 56
- DAY 22 — Ordering Drinks and an Appetizer — 58
- DAY 23 — The Waiter Returns — 60
- DAY 24 — The Food Arrives — 62
- DAY 25 — A Lovely Meal — 64

Contents

SECTION 6
Airport
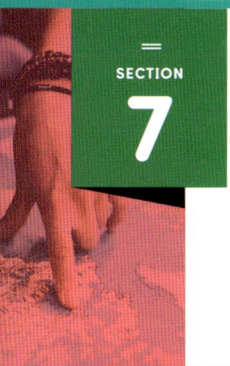
- DAY 26 Check-in — 68
- DAY 27 Security — 70
- DAY 28 Boarding — 72
- DAY 29 The Flight — 74
- DAY 30 Immigration (Arrival) — 76

SECTION 7
Travel

- DAY 31 Car Rental — 80
- DAY 32 Hotel Check-In — 82
- DAY 33 The Hotel Concierge — 84
- DAY 34 Sightseeing — 86
- DAY 35 Hotel Check-out — 88

SECTION 8
Health

- DAY 36 Exercise — 92
- DAY 37 An Accident — 94
- DAY 38 In the Doctor's Office — 96
- DAY 39 The Examination — 98
- DAY 40 At the Pharmacy — 100

SECTION 9
Special Occasions
- DAY 41 Planning a Party — 104
- DAY 42 Other Plans — 106
- DAY 43 Party Preparation — 108
- DAY 44 Wrapping a Gift — 110
- DAY 45 At the Party — 112

SECTION 10
Descriptions

- DAY 46 Getting a Haircut — 116
- DAY 47 Lost and Found — 118
- DAY 48 A Cooking Lesson — 120
- DAY 49 The Date — 122
- DAY 50 A Movie Discussion — 124

Answer Key — 126

SECTION 1

New Neighbors

새로운 이웃 만나기

Scan for Preview

DAY 1 Introductions
소개

DAY 2 The Visit
방문

DAY 3 Occupations
직업

DAY 4 School
학교

DAY 5 Saying Goodbye
작별 인사

NEW NEIGHBORS

DAY 1

소개
Introductions

▬ KEY VOCABULARY

neighbor	이웃(사람)
toward	~쪽으로, ~을 향하여
shake hands	악수하다
hometown	고향
plan	계획
schedule	스케줄, 일정
husband	남편
invite	초대하다

▬ KEY EXPRESSIONS

- **Please call me ...** ~ 라고 부르세요.
  - **Please call me** Kim.
    Kim이라고 부르세요.
  - **Please call me** Bill.
    Bill이라고 부르세요.

- **... is my hometown.**
  ~ 이 제 고향입니다.
  - Austin **is my hometown.**
    오스틴이 제 고향입니다.
  - Chicago **is my hometown.**
    시카고가 제 고향입니다.

- **What are your plans ...?**
  ~ 에 무슨 계획이 있으세요?
  - **What are your plans** this evening**?**
    오늘 저녁에 무슨 계획 있으세요?
  - **What are your plans** this Friday**?**
    이번 금요일에는 무슨 계획 있으세요?

- **Is around ... OK?**
  ~ 쯤 어떠세요?
  - **Is around** 8:00 **OK?**
    8시쯤 어떠세요?
  - **Is around** 7 a.m. **OK?**
    오전 7시쯤 어떠세요?

▬ STUDY TIP

처음 만나는 사람에게 하는 친근한 인사:

Nice to meet you.
Glad to meet you.
Pleased to meet you.
It's a pleasure to meet you.
It's very nice to meet you.

대화를 들어보세요. 그런 다음 롤플레잉을 해보세요.

Mary sees her new ¹neighbor.
Mary는 새로운 이웃을 만난다.

They walk ²toward each other...
서로에게 가까이 다가간다.

...and ³shake hands.
그리고 악수를 한다.

Mary asks where Kim is from.
Mary는 Kim이 어디 출신인지 물어본다.

They talk.
그들은 이야기를 나눈다.

Mary asks about Kim's evening ⁶schedule.
Mary는 Kim의 저녁 스케줄을 물어본다.

Mary ⁸invites Kim to her house.
Mary는 Kim을 집으로 초대한다.

They say good-bye.
그들은 작별 인사를 나눈다.

MATCHING

올바른 영영 뜻을 B열에서 찾아 A열 옆에 쓰세요.

A	B
_____ 1. hometown	a. to ask someone to come to an event 초대하다
_____ 2. husband	b. a person who lives close to you 이웃
_____ 3. invite	c. the town you were born in or grew up in 고향
_____ 4. neighbor	d. a list of things to do and the time you should do them 일정
_____ 5. schedule	e. a man someone is married to 남편

CONVERSATION

올바른 영어 표현으로 쓰고 말해보세요.

Nice to 1 _____ you. I'm Mary Smith.
만나서 반가워요. Mary Smith에요.

Hello.
Hi.

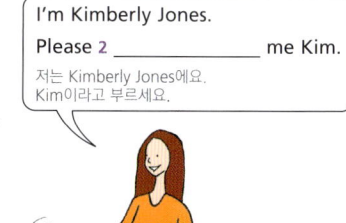

I'm Kimberly Jones. Please 2 _____ me Kim.
저는 Kimberly Jones에요. Kim이라고 부르세요.

Where are you from?

Atlanta. But I was living in 3 _____ for the last four years.
애틀랜타에요. 하지만 지난 4년 동안 시카고에 살았죠.

Yes, Austin is my 4 _____.
예, 오스틴이 제 고향입니다.

Are you from here?

That's nice.

What are your 5 _____ this evening?
오늘 저녁에 무슨 계획 있으세요?

Nothing special.

Come have coffee with my 6 _____ and me. Is around 8:00 OK?
우리 집에서 저와 남편이랑 8시쯤 커피 마시는 거 어때요?

That sounds great, thanks.

Well, see you tonight!

OK. See you then.

DAY 2

NEW NEIGHBORS

방문
The Visit

KEY VOCABULARY

pleasure	기쁨, 즐거움
hang up	걸다
introduce	소개하다
greet	맞다, 환영하다
living room	거실
lovely	사랑스러운, 아름다운
look around	둘러보다
offer	제안하다, 권하다
choice	선택(하는 행동)

KEY EXPRESSIONS

- **Thanks for …** ~ 해주셔서 고마워요.
  - **Thanks for** inviting me. 초대해주셔서 고마워요.
  - **Thanks for** holding the door. 문 잡아주셔서 감사해요.

- **May I take …?** ~ 받아드릴까요?
  - **May I take** your jacket? 재킷 받아드릴까요?
  - **May I take** your scarf? 스카프 받아드릴까요?

- **Let's go into …** ~ 로 가시죠.
  - **Let's go into** the living room. 거실로 들어가시죠.
  - **Let's go into** the dining room. 식당으로 가시죠.

- **Would you like …?** ~ 하시겠습니까?
  - **Would you like** anything to drink? 마실 것 좀 드릴까요?
  - **Would you like** a cup of coffee? 커피 한 잔 드릴까요?

STUDY TIP

'제안하다'라는 뜻을 가진 단어

offer: 제안하다, 제공하다
- 가지고 있는 것을 제공한다는 뉘앙스
  He offered me a drink.
  그가 나에게 음료를 권했다.

suggest: 제안하다, 권장하다
- 상대방이 할지 안 할지는 모르겠지만, 하면 좋겠다고 권장하는 의미
  I suggest that you attend a party.
  당신이 파티에 참석하는 게 좋겠어요.

propose: 제안하다
- suggest보다 격식 있게 표현할 때 주로 사용
  I propose a toast to our success!
  우리의 성공을 위해 건배를 제안합니다!

대화를 들어보세요. 그런 다음 롤플레잉을 해보세요.

Thanks for inviting me. 초대해주셔서 고마워요.
Hi, Kim! Please come in! Kim, 안녕하세요! 어서 오세요!
Our [1]pleasure. 저희가 기쁜걸요.

Kim arrives at John and Mary's house.
Kim은 John과 Mary의 집에 도착한다.

May I take your jacket? 재킷 받아 드릴까요?
Sure. Thank you. 그러죠, 고맙습니다.

Mary [2]hangs up Kim's jacket.
Mary는 Kim의 재킷을 옷걸이에 걸어놓는다.

John, meet Kim, our new neighbor! John, Kim과 인사하세요. 새로운 이웃이에요!
coat hooks 코트 걸이

Mary [3]introduces John to Kim.
Mary는 John을 Kim에게 소개한다.

Hello, Kim. Nice to meet you. 안녕하세요, Kim. 만나서 반가워요.
Thanks. Good to meet you, too. 고마워요. 저도 만나서 반갑습니다.

John and Kim [4]greet each other and shake hands.
John과 Kim은 서로 인사하고 악수를 나눈다.

Let's go into the [5]living room. 거실로 들어가시죠.
Thank you very much. 고맙습니다.
Your home is [6]lovely. 집이 좋군요.

They go into another room.
그들은 다른 방으로 들어간다.

Kim [7]looks around the house.
Kim은 집을 둘러본다.

Kim, would you like anything to drink? Kim, 마실 것 좀 드릴까요?
Yes, please. 예, 고맙습니다.

We have coffee, juice, soda... 커피, 주스, 탄산수가...
Orange juice sounds good, thanks. 오렌지주스가 좋겠군요, 고마워요.
I'll have some too, dear. 여보, 나도 좀.

Mary [8]offers Kim a drink...
Mary는 Kim에게 마실 것을 권한다.

...and tells her the [9]choices.
그리고 그녀에게 고른 것을 이야기한다.

MATCHING

올바른 영영 뜻을 B열에서 찾아 A열 옆에 쓰세요.

A

_____ 1. greet
_____ 2. introduce
_____ 3. living room
_____ 4. look around
_____ 5. lovely

B

a. to tell a person's name for the first time 소개하다
b. the state of being beautiful 사랑스러운
c. to explore a place 둘러보다
d. a room that is used for relaxing 거실
e. to say hello to someone 맞다

CONVERSATION

올바른 영어 표현으로 쓰고 말해보세요.

1 _____ for inviting me. 초대해주셔서 고마워요.

Hi, Kim! Please 2 _____ in! Kim, 안녕하세요! 어서 오세요!

Our pleasure.

May I 3 _____ your jacket? 재킷 받아 드릴까요?

Sure. Thank you.

John, meet Kim, our new 4 _____! John, Kim과 인사하세요. 새로운 이웃이에요!

Hello, Kim. Nice to meet you.

Thanks. 5 _____ to meet you, too. 고마워요. 저도 만나서 반갑습니다.

Let's 6 _____ into the living room. 거실로 들어가시죠.

Thank you very much.

Your home is 7 _____. 집이 좋군요.

Kim, would you like anything to 8 _____? Kim, 마실 것 좀 드릴까요?

Yes, please.

We have coffee, juice, soda...

Orange juice sounds good, thanks.

I'll 9 _____ some too, dear. 여보, 나도 좀.

DAY 3
NEW NEIGHBORS

직업
Occupations

▬ KEY VOCABULARY

company	회사
enjoy (syn. like)	즐기다
engineer	엔지니어
bring	가져오다
accounts	회계부
part-time	파트타임
describe	말하다, 묘사하다

▬ KEY EXPRESSIONS

- **How do you like ...?**
  ~이 마음에 드세요?
  - **How do you like** Austin?
    오스틴이 마음에 드세요?
  - **How do you like** New York?
    뉴욕이 마음에 드세요?

- **I work for ...** 저는 ~에서 일해요.
  - **I work for** an Internet company.
    저는 인터넷 회사에서 일해요.
  - **I work for** Disney.
    저는 디즈니에서 일해요.

- **I'm ... (직업)** 저는 ~에요.
  - **I'm** an engineer.
    저는 엔지니어에요.
  - **I'm** a plumber.
    저는 배관공이에요.

▬ STUDY TIP

직장을 물을 때 사용할 수 있는 표현:

What do you do?
어떤 일을 하세요?
= What do you do for a living?

What does she/he do?
그녀/그는 어떤 일을 하나요?
= What does she/he do for a living?

보통 'What is your job?' 보다는
'What do you do?' 가 직업을 묻는 표현으로
자주 쓰인다.

대화를 들어보세요. 그런 다음 롤플레잉을 해보세요.

John offers Kim a seat.
John은 Kim에게 앉으라고 권한다.

John and Kim sit down.
John과 Kim은 자리에 앉는다.

John asks Kim about her job.
John은 Kim에게 그녀의 직업에 대해 물어본다.

John asks if Kim [2]enjoys her work.
John과 Kim에게 일에 만족하는지 물어본다.

John tells Kim about his work.
John은 Kim에게 자신의 일에 대해 이야기 해준다.

Mary [4]brings the drinks...
Mary가 마실 것을 가져온다.

...and sits down.
그리고 자리에 앉는다.

Mary [7]describes her job at the bank.
Mary는 은행에서 하는 자신의 일에 대해 얘기한다.

MATCHING

올바른 영영 뜻을 B열에서 찾아 A열 옆에 쓰세요.

A

_____ 1. company
_____ 2. describe
_____ 3. engineer
_____ 4. enjoy
_____ 5. part-time

B

a. a business 회사
b. to tell how something looks, smells, etc. 묘사하다
c. to like something 즐기다
d. working only part of each day or week 파트타임
e. a person who designs machines 엔지니어

CONVERSATION

올바른 영어 표현으로 쓰고 말해보세요.

Please 1 _____ down.
앉으세요.

Thank you.

2 _____ do you like Austin?
오스틴이 마음에 드세요?

It's very 3 _____!
매우 좋아요!

What do you do?

I work for an Internet 4 _____.
인터넷 회사에서 일해요.

Do you like it?

Not really. I'm looking for a new 5 _____. What about you?
그렇지 않아요. 새로운 일자리를 알아보고 있어요. 당신은요?

I'm an 6 _____.
저는 엔지니어에요.

Oh, that's 7 _____.
오, 흥미롭군요.

Here you are.

Thank you. Do you 8 _____, Mary?
고마워요. Mary, 당신도 직장에 다니시나요?

Yes, I work at a 9 _____.
네, 저는 은행에서 일해요.

What do you do there?

I work in accounts, but only 10 _____.
회계 부서에서 일하고 있지만, 파트타임이에요.

SECTION 1 NEW NEIGHBORS

NEW NEIGHBORS
DAY 4 — 학교 / School

KEY VOCABULARY

business	경영학
MBA (Master of Business Administration)	경영학 석사
pet	쓰다듬다, 어루만지다
major	전공
college	대학, 칼리지
education	학력, 교육
cousin	사촌, 친척
sophomore	2학년생
bathroom (syn. restroom)	화장실

KEY EXPRESSIONS

- **I majored in …** 저는 ~ 을 전공했어요.
  - **I majored in** math. 저는 수학을 전공했어요.
  - **I majored in** journalism. 저는 언론학을 전공했어요.

- **My … is a … there.** 제 ~ 가 거기 ~ 입니다.
  - **My** cousin **is a** sophomore **there.** 제 사촌이 그 대학 2학년입니다.
  - **My** younger brother **is a** junior **there.** 제 남동생이 거기 3학년입니다.

- **May I use …?** ~ 를 써도 될까요?
  - **May I use** your bathroom? 화장실 좀 써도 될까요?
  - **May I use** your phone? 당신의 전화기를 써도 될까요?

STUDY TIP

'Where did you go to school?'에 대한 다양한 대답:
I went to Brighton University.
I attended Brighton University.
I graduated from Brighton University.
I studied at Brighton University.

대화를 들어보세요. 그런 다음 롤플레잉을 해보세요.

I am also studying part-time. Oh! This is Sam.
저는 파트타임으로 공부도 하고 있어요. 아! 여기 Sam이에요.

Mary and John's cat comes in.
Mary와 John의 고양이가 들어온다.

[1]Business. I'm getting an [2]MBA.
경영학 전공이에요. 경영학 석사를 따려고 해요.

He's very cute! What are you studying?
고양이가 무척 귀엽군요! 당신은 무엇을 공부하세요?

Kim [3]pets Sam.
Kim은 Sam을 쓰다듬는다.

What was your [4]major in [5]college?
대학에서는 무엇을 전공하셨어요?

Accounting. How about you?
회계학이에요. 당신은요?

Kim asks Mary's major.
Kim은 Mary의 전공을 물어본다.

I majored in math.
저는 수학을 전공했어요.

Kim talks about her [6]education.
Kim은 자신의 학력에 대해 이야기 한다.

Where did you go to school, Kim?
Kim, 당신은 어느 학교에 다니셨어요?

I went to Brighton University.
저는 브라이튼 대학에 다녔어요.

The cat walks over to John…
고양이가 John에게로 걸어간다.

Really!? My [7]cousin is a [8]sophomore there.
정말요? 내 사촌이 그 대학 2학년인데.

Wow! Small world!
와! 세상 좁군요!

…and John picks him up.
그러자 John은 Sam을 들어 올린다.

Excuse me. May I use your [9]bathroom?
실례지만, 화장실 좀 써도 될까요?

Of course.
물론이죠.

Kim puts down her drink.
Kim은 자신의 주스를 테이블에 놓는다.

It's down the hall on the right.
복도를 따라가면 오른쪽에 있어요.

Thanks a lot.
고마워요.

Mary shows Kim to the bathroom.
Mary는 Kim에게 화장실을 안내한다.

MATCHING

올바른 영영 뜻을 B열에서 찾아 A열 옆에 쓰세요.

A
1. bathroom
2. college
3. cousin
4. major
5. sophomore

B
a. the main subject of study 전공
b. a place to take a shower or use the toilet 화장실
c. the daughter or son of your aunt or uncle 사촌
d. a student in the second year of high school or college 2학년생
e. a school you go to after high school 대학

CONVERSATION

올바른 영어 표현으로 쓰고 말해보세요.

I am also studying part-time. Oh! This is Sam.

He's very cute! What are you 1 _____?
고양이가 무척 귀엽군요! 당신은 무엇을 공부하세요?

2 _____.
I'm getting an MBA.
경영학 전공이에요. 경영학 석사를 따려고 해요.

What was your 3 _____ in college?
대학에서는 무엇을 전공하셨어요?

Accounting. How about you?

I majored in 4 _____.
저는 수학을 전공했어요.

Where did you go to 5 _____, Kim?
Kim, 당신은 어느 학교에 다니셨어요?

I went to Brighton University.

Really!? My cousin is a 6 _____ there.
정말요? 내 사촌이 그 대학 2학년인데.

Wow! Small world!

Excuse me. 7 _____ I use your bathroom?
실례지만, 화장실 좀 써도 될까요?

Of course.

It's down the hall on the right.

Thanks a lot.

NEW NEIGHBORS
DAY 5

작별 인사
Saying Goodbye

KEY VOCABULARY

guest (syn. visitor)	손님
notice	~을 의식하다, ~을 알다
go to bed	자다, 취침하다
jog	조깅하다
night owl	올빼미 같은 사람
strawberry jam	딸기잼
jar	(특히 잼, 꿀 등을 담아두는) 병

KEY EXPRESSIONS

- **Can I get you …?** ~ 드릴까요?
  - **Can I get you** anything else?
    뭘 좀 드릴까요?
  - **Can I get you** a drink?
    마실 것을 드릴까요?

- **I'll get you …** ~ 를 드릴게요.
  - **I'll get you** a jar.
    한 병 드릴게요.
  - **I'll get you** a napkin.
    냅킨을 드릴게요.

- **It was … to … you.** 당신을 ~ 해서 ~ 했어요.
  - **It was** nice **to** meet **you.**
    만나서 반가웠어요.
  - **It was** great **to** see **you** again.
    다시 만나서 반가웠어요.

- **I hope …** ~ 해주세요. / ~ 를 바랍니다.
  - **I hope** you can visit me sometime.
    언제 우리 집에 방문해주세요.
  - **I hope** you can come to the meetup.
    당신이 그 모임에 오기를 바랍니다.

STUDY TIP

영어로는 저녁형 인간을 night owl(올빼미 같은 사람), 아침형 인간을 morning lark(아침 종달새) 라고 한다.
동물 대신에 night person(저녁형 인간), morning person(아침형 인간) 이라고도 한다.

대화를 들어보세요. 그런 다음 롤플레잉을 해보세요.

Mary checks on her ¹guest.
Mary는 손님에게 필요한 것이 있는지 물어본다.

Can I get you anything else? 뭘 좀 드릴까요?
No, thank you. 아니요, 고맙습니다.

Kim ²notices the time.
Kim은 시간을 확인한다.

Why so soon? 왜 벌써 가세요?
Actually, I should go now. 사실은 지금 가야 해요.

I usually ³go to bed early. I like to ⁴jog in the morning.
저는 일찍 잠자리에 들거든요. 아침에 조깅을 하고 있습니다.

I can't do that. I'm not a morning person.
전 그렇지 못해요. 아침형 인간이 아니라서.

We're both ⁵night owls. Say, Kim, do you like ⁶strawberry jam?
우리는 올빼미 같죠. 그런데 Kim, 딸기잼 좋아하세요?

They stand up...
그들은 자리에서 일어난다.

...and walk to the door.
출입문으로 걸어간다.

Yes. I love it! 예, 좋아해요!
I made some last week. I'll get you a ⁷jar. 지난주에 좀 만들었는데, 한 병 드릴게요.

Thanks. It was nice to meet you. 고맙습니다. 만나서 반가웠어요.
Thanks for coming. We enjoyed meeting you, too. 와 주셔서 고맙습니다. 우리도 만나서 반가웠어요.

Mary goes to the kitchen.
Mary는 부엌으로 간다.

Kim puts on her jacket.
Kim은 재킷을 입는다.

Thank you very much! I hope you can visit me sometime, too. 고맙습니다! 언제 우리 집도 방문해주세요.
That would be nice. 그러면 좋겠군요.

Good night. 안녕히 계세요.
Good night. 잘 가세요.
See you! 다시 만나요!

Mary gives the jam to Kim.
Mary는 잼을 Kim에게 건넨다.

Kim walks out the door.
Kim은 문밖으로 걸어 나간다.

MATCHING

올바른 영영 뜻을 B열에서 찾아 A열 옆에 쓰세요.

A	B
_____ 1. go to bed	a. to run slowly often as a form of exercise 조깅하다
_____ 2. guest	b. a person who is visiting from another place 손님
_____ 3. jog	c. someone who enjoys staying up late 올빼미 같은 사람
_____ 4. night owl	d. to sleep 취침하다
_____ 5. strawberry jam	e. a jelly made from strawberries 딸기잼

CONVERSATION

올바른 영어 표현으로 쓰고 말해보세요.

Can I 1 _____ you anything else? 뭘 좀 드릴까요?
No, thank you.

Why so 2 _____? 왜 벌써 가세요?
Actually, I should go now.

I usually go to 3 _____ early. I like to jog in the morning.
저는 일찍 잠자리에 들거든요. 아침에 조깅을 하고 있습니다.

I can't do that. I'm not a morning person.

We're both 4 _____. Say, Kim, do you like strawberry jam?
우리는 올빼미 같죠. 그런데 Kim, 딸기잼 좋아하세요?

Yes. I love it!
I made some last week. I'll get you a 5 _____.
지난주에 좀 만들었는데, 한 병 드릴게요.

Thanks. It was nice to meet you.
Thanks for coming. We enjoyed meeting you, too.

Thank you very much! I hope you can 6 _____ me sometime, too.
고맙습니다! 언제 우리 집도 방문해주세요.
That would be nice.

Good 7 _____. 안녕히 계세요.
Good night.
See you!

SECTION 1 NEW NEIGHBORS 17

Scan for Preview

DAY 6   Women's Clothing
여성복

DAY 7   Sizes and Trying Things On
사이즈와 입어보기

DAY 8   Men's Clothing
남성복

DAY 9   Paying at the Counter
카운터에서 계산하기

DAY 10   Electronics
전자제품

SHOPPING
DAY 6
여성복
Women's Clothing

KEY VOCABULARY

salesperson	판매원
point to	가리키다
beige	베이지색
length	길이
perfect (syn. excellent)	완벽한, 꼭 맞는
medium	중간의
find	찾다, 발견하다
try on	입어보다
fitting room	탈의실

KEY EXPRESSIONS

- **I'm looking for …** ~을 찾고 있어요.
  - **I'm looking for** some spring clothes.
    봄옷을 찾고 있어요.
  - **I'm looking for** a purse.
    지갑을 찾고 있어요.

- **What … would you like?** 어떤 ~을 원하세요?
  - **What** color skirt **would you like?**
    어떤 색의 치마를 원하세요?
  - **What** size blouse **would you like?**
    어떤 사이즈의 블라우스를 원하세요?

- **How about …?** ~는 어때요?
  - **How about** this one?
    이건 어때요?
  - **How about** this dress?
    이 드레스는 어때요?

- **Would you like to …?** ~하실래요?
  - **Would you like to** try these on?
    입어보실래요?
  - **Would you like to** see some products?
    몇 가지 상품을 보실래요?

STUDY TIP

외국에서는 의류와 신발 사이즈가 우리나라와는 다르다. 여성 의류의 경우 사이즈 XS은 0, 2, S는 4와 6, M은 8과 10, L은 12와 14로 표기한다.

대화를 들어보세요. 그런 다음 롤플레잉을 해보세요.

The ¹salesperson greets Julia.
판매원이 Julia에게 인사한다.

The salesperson ²points to the skirts.
판매원이 스커트를 가리킨다.

Julia asks for a beige skirt.
Julia는 베이지색 스커트를 요구한다.

The salesperson looks through the skirts.
판매원이 스커트를 살펴본다.

The salesperson takes a skirt off the rack.
판매원이 스커트를 옷걸이에서 꺼낸다.

Julia points to the display.
Julia는 디스플레이를 가리킨다.

The salesperson ⁷finds Julia a light blue blouse.
판매원은 Julia에게 하늘색 블라우스를 찾아 준다.

Julia takes the blouse from the salesperson.
Julia는 판매원에게 블라우스를 받는다.

MATCHING

올바른 영영 뜻을 B열에서 찾아 A열 옆에 쓰세요.

A	B
_____ 1. length	a. a room in a shop where you can put on clothes 탈의실
_____ 2. perfect	b. exactly right for someone or something 완벽한
_____ 3. medium	c. the measurement of something from end to end 길이
_____ 4. find	d. being in the middle between size large and size small 중간의
_____ 5. fitting room	e. to discover 찾다

CONVERSATION

올바른 영어 표현으로 쓰고 말해보세요.

May I help you?

Yes. I'm looking for some 1 _____.
예, 봄옷을 찾고 있어요.

Well, we have some new skirts and blouses.

That sounds 2 _____.
좋아요.

What 3 _____ skirt would you like?
어떤 색의 치마를 원하세요?

Maybe a beige one.

What size are you 4 _____?
어떤 사이즈를 찾으세요?

Size 8.

Here's one in size 8. Is the length all right?

Yes.

Do you have this style blouse in 5 _____?
이 스타일의 블라우스로 하늘색은 없나요?

How 6 _____ this one?
이건 어때요?

Perfect! Do you have a 7 _____ one?
아주 좋군요! 중간 사이즈 있나요?

Here's a medium. Would you like to 8 _____ these on?
여기 중간 사이즈에요. 입어보실래요?

Yes, please. Where are the fitting rooms?

Right this way.

SHOPPING
DAY 7
사이즈와 입어보기
Sizes and Trying Things On

— KEY VOCABULARY

fit	(모양 크기가 어떤 사람 사물에) 맞다
pair	짝, 똑같은 종류의 두 물건
sandal	샌들
counter	계산대, 판매대
style	스타일
popular	인기 있는, 대중적인
tight	꽉 조이는

— KEY EXPRESSIONS

- **I'd like ...** ~를 원해요.
  - **I'd like** a pair of sandals.
    샌들을 원해요.
  - **I'd like** two of these.
    이것 두 개를 원해요.

- **What ... do you wear?** 어떤 ~을 입으세요?
  - **What** size **do you wear?**
    어떤 사이즈를 입으세요? / 신으세요?
  - **What** length **do you** usually **wear?**
    보통 어떤 길이를 입으세요?

- **Why don't you ...?** ~ 하는 게 어때요?
  - **Why don't you** try the 8 first?
    사이즈 8을 먼저 신어보시겠어요?
  - **Why don't you** try on the blue one?
    파란색을 입어보는 게 어때요?

- **They feel ...** ~하네요.
  - **They feel** tight.
    이건 꽉 조이네요.
  - **They feel** uncomfortable.
    불편하네요.

— STUDY TIP

미국의 여성 신발 사이즈:

한국 (mm)	230	235	240	245	250	255
미국	6	6.5	7	7.5	8	8.5

대화를 들어보세요. 그런 다음 롤플레잉을 해보세요.

The blouse looks great but the skirt is too big. Can I try a smaller one?
블라우스는 괜찮은데 스커트는 너무 크네요. 작은 거로 입어볼 수 있나요?

Of course. I'll get one for you.
물론이죠. 드릴게요.

curtain 커튼

Julia tries on the blouse and skirt.
Julia는 블라우스와 스커트를 입어본다.

Did that size ¹fit better?
그 사이즈가 더 잘 맞나요?

Yes, thank you. I'll take them.
그러네요. 고마워요. 이걸로 할게요.

Julia decides to buy the skirt and blouse.
Julia는 스커트와 블라우스를 사기로 결정한다.

Will you need anything else today?
다른 것은 필요치 않으세요?

Yes. I'd like a ²pair of ³sandals, too.
샌들도 사야겠네요.

This ⁵style is ⁶popular.
이 스타일이 유행이에요.

Wow! Those are really cute!
와! 정말 예쁘네요!

The salesperson puts the clothes on the ⁴counter.
판매원은 옷을 카운터에 올려놓는다.

The salesperson shows Julia some sandals.
판매원은 Julia에게 샌들을 보여준다.

What size do you wear?
어떤 사이즈를 신으시죠?

I'm not sure. Maybe an 8 or 8 and a half.
모르겠네요. 아마, 8 또는 8.5 정도일 거예요.

Here you are. Why don't you try the 8 first?
여기 있어요. 사이즈 8을 먼저 신어보시겠어요?

Julia tells her shoe size.
Julia는 신발 사이즈를 말한다.

The salesperson brings two boxes.
판매원은 신발 상자 두 개를 가져온다.

They feel ⁷tight.
이건 꽉 조이네요.

Here's the 8 and a half.
그럼 8.5를 신어보세요.

These fit much better. Thank you for your help.
이게 훨씬 잘 맞네요. 도와줘서 고마워요.

You're welcome.
천만에요.

mirror 거울

Julia puts on a shoe.
Julia는 신발 한 짝을 신어본다.

Julia is happy with the other sandals.
Julia는 다른 샌들에 만족해한다.

MATCHING

올바른 영영 뜻을 B열에서 찾아 A열 옆에 쓰세요.

A		B
_____ 1. fit		a. a person's way of dressing 스타일
_____ 2. pair		b. to be the right size (모양 크기가 어떤 사람 사물에) 맞다
_____ 3. popular		c. a shoe with straps and an open toe 샌들
_____ 4. sandal		d. liked by many people 인기 있는
_____ 5. style		e. an item with two parts 짝

CONVERSATION

올바른 영어 표현으로 쓰고 말해보세요.

The blouse looks great but the skirt is too big. Can I 1 _____ a smaller one?
블라우스는 괜찮은데 스커트는 너무 크네요. 작은 거로 입어볼 수 있나요?

Of course. I'll get one for you.

Did that size 2 _____ better?
그 사이즈가 더 잘 맞나요?

Yes, thank you. I'll take them.

Will you need anything else today?

Yes. I'd like a pair of 3 _____, too.
샌들도 사야겠네요.

This style is 4 _____.
이 스타일이 유행이에요.

Wow! Those are really cute!

What 5 _____ do you wear?
어떤 사이즈를 신으시죠?

I'm not sure. Maybe an 8 or 8 and a half.

Here you are. Why don't you try the 8 first?

They feel 6 _____.
이건 꽉 조이네요.

Here's the 8 and a half.

These fit much 7 _____. Thank you for your help.
이게 훨씬 잘 맞네요. 도와줘서 고마워요.

You're welcome.

SHOPPING
DAY 8
남성복
Men's Clothing

▬ KEY VOCABULARY

jeans	청바지
waist	허리
choose	고르다
sale	세일, 할인 판매
cotton	면직물
polyester	폴리에스테르(섬유)
material	재료
rub	문지르다
hand	건네주다, 넘겨주다

▬ KEY EXPRESSIONS

- **I need ...** 저는 ~ 가 필요합니다.
  - **I need** a pair of jeans.
    청바지가 필요합니다.
  - **I need** a pair of pants.
    바지 한 벌이 필요합니다.

- **What ... of ... are you looking for?**
  어떤 ~ 의 ~ 을 찾으세요?
  - **What** kind **of** jeans **are you looking for?**
    어떤 청바지를 찾고 계세요?
  - **What** color **of** blouse **are you looking for?**
    어떤 색상의 블라우스를 찾으세요?

- **Do you have ...?** ~ 있나요?
  - **Do you have** Diorgano jeans?
    디어가노 청바지 있나요?
  - **Do you have** corduroy pants?
    코르덴 바지 있나요?

- **I'll take ...** ~ 로 할게요.
  - **I'll take** a large one.
    큰 것으로 할게요.
  - **I'll take** a medium one.
    중간 사이즈로 할게요.

▬ STUDY TIP

미국의 남성 하의 사이즈:

사이즈	XS	S	M	L
인치	28-29	30-31	32-33	34-35
미국	34	36	38	40

대화를 들어보세요. 그런 다음 롤플레잉을 해보세요.

Peter goes into a men's clothing store.
Peter는 남성복 가게에 들어간다.

The salesman and Peter stand by the jeans display.
판매원과 Peter는 청바지 진열대 옆에 서 있다.

Peter tells the salesman his size.
Peter는 판매원에게 옷 사이즈를 얘기한다.

He ³chooses a pair of jeans.
그는 청바지를 고른다.

The salesman tells Peter about a sale.
판매원은 Peter에게 할인 판매에 대해 이야기 한다.

Peter asks about the ⁷material.
Peter는 소재에 대해 묻는다.

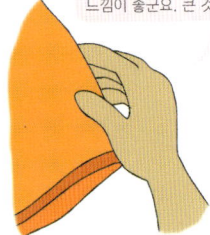

Peter ⁸rubs the material.
Peter는 소재를 문질러본다.

The salesman ⁹hands Peter a large T-shirt.
판매원은 Peter에게 큰 사이즈의 티셔츠를 건넨다.

MATCHING

올바른 영영 뜻을 B열에서 찾아 A열 옆에 쓰세요.

A	B
_____ 1. choose	a. to move something back and forth on a surface 문지르다
_____ 2. cotton	b. soft white plant fibers used to make cloth 면직물
_____ 3. jeans	c. the middle part of the body 허리
_____ 4. rub	d. pants that are made from denim 청바지
_____ 5. waist	e. to select 고르다

CONVERSATION

올바른 영어 표현으로 쓰고 말해보세요.

Good afternoon. May I help you?

Yes, please. I 1 _____ a pair of jeans.
고맙습니다. 청바지가 필요합니다.

What kind of jeans are you 2 _____ for?
어떤 청바지를 찾고 계세요?

Do you have Diorgano jeans?

Yes, we do.

What 3 _____ do you wear?
어떤 사이즈 입으세요?

I wear size 33 4 _____ and 34 length.
허리 33과 길이 34 사이즈를 입습니다.

These should 5 _____ you.
이것이 맞으시겠군요.

Thank you for your help.

We have a 6 _____ on T-shirts this week.
이번 주는 티셔츠를 할인 가격에 팔고 있습니다.

That's great!

Are these 100% 7 _____?
이건 면 100%인가요?

No, they're 80% cotton and 20% polyester.

That feels 8 _____. I'll take a large one, please.
느낌이 좋군요. 큰 것으로 할게요.

Can I 9 _____ you anything else?
다른 것은 필요 없나요?

No, thank you.

SHOPPING
DAY 9
카운터에서 계산하기
Paying at the Counter

— KEY VOCABULARY

cash	현금
payment	지불, 지급
total	합계, 총
swipe	(신용카드 같은 전자 카드를) 긁다
credit card	신용 카드
sign	서명하다
receipt	영수증
exchange	교환하다
leave (ant. arrive)	떠나다

— KEY EXPRESSIONS

- **Your total is …** 총 ~ 예요.
  - **Your total is** $65.
    총 65달러예요.
  - **Your total is** $251.23.
    총 251.23달러예요.

- **Can I use …?** ~ 를 사용할 수 있을까요?
  - **Can I use** your pen please?
    펜 좀 쓸 수 있을까요?
  - **Can I use** your pencil please?
    연필을 쓸 수 있을까요?

- **Here's …** 여기 ~ 있습니다.
  - **Here's** your card and the receipt.
    여기 카드와 영수증이 있습니다.
  - **Here's** your receipt.
    여기 영수증이 있습니다.

- **If you need to …, just …**
  ~ 가 필요하시면 그냥 ~ 하세요.
  - **If you need to** exchange anything, **just** bring it back with your receipt.
    교환할 것이 있으시면, 물건과 영수증을 가져오세요.
  - **If you need to** return this, **just** bring it along with your credit card.
    환불이 필요하시면, 카드와 함께 가져오세요.

— STUDY TIP

총액을 말할 때 사용할 수 있는 표현:

Your total is $65.
The total is going to be $65.
That comes to $65.
It is 65 dollars in total.

대화를 들어보세요. 그런 다음 롤플레잉을 해보세요.

The salesman and Peter go to the counter.
판매원과 Peter는 카운터로 간다.

The salesman takes Peter's ²payment.
판매원은 Peter의 카드를 받는다.

The salesman ⁴swipes Peter's ⁵credit card.
판매원은 Peter의 신용카드를 처리한다.

Peter signs the ⁷receipt.
Peter는 영수증에 서명한다.

Peter takes his receipt and credit card.
Peter는 영수증과 신용카드를 받는다.

The salesman puts Peter's clothes in a bag.
판매원은 Peter의 옷을 가방에 넣는다.

The salesman gives Peter the bag.
판매원은 Peter에게 가방을 건넨다.

Peter ⁹leaves the store.
Peter는 가게를 나선다.

MATCHING

올바른 영영 뜻을 B열에서 찾아 A열 옆에 쓰세요.

A

_____ 1. cash
_____ 2. exchange
_____ 3. receipt
_____ 4. sign
_____ 5. total

B

a. a piece of paper that shows what you bought 영수증
b. to write your name 서명하다
c. the amount when all items are added together 합계
d. paper money or coins 현금
e. to return an item and get a new one 교환하다

CONVERSATION

올바른 영어 표현으로 쓰고 말해보세요.

Would you like to 1 _____ your clothes?
구입하신 옷 입어보시겠어요?

That's OK. I'll just take them.

Your 3 _____ is $65.
총 65달러에요.

Here's your card and the 5 _____.
여기 카드와 영수증이 있습니다.

Thank you.

Here you are.

Thank you.

Will that be 2 _____. or card?
현금으로 하시겠어요, 아니면 카드로 하시겠어요?

Card.

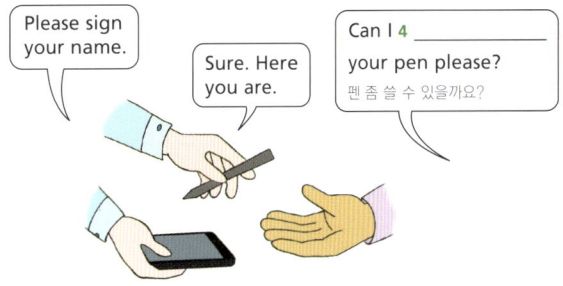

Please sign your name.

Sure. Here you are.

Can I 4 _____ your pen please?
펜 좀 쓸 수 있을까요?

It you need to 6 _____ anything, just bring it back with your receipt.
교환할 것이 있으시면, 물건과 영수증을 가져오세요.

Have a nice day, sir. Please 7 _____ again.
좋은 하루 되시고, 또 방문해 주세요.

Thank you. Good-bye.

SECTION 2 SHOPPING

SHOPPING
DAY 10

전자제품
Electronics

— KEY VOCABULARY

enter	들어가다, 들어오다
electronics shop	전자제품 가게
salesclerk	점원, 판매원
expensive (ant. cheap)	비싼
feature	특징, 특성
warranty	보증
free	무료의
pay for	대금을 지불하다

— KEY EXPRESSIONS

- **Do you sell …?** ~ 파나요?
  - **Do you sell** cameras?
    카메라 파나요?
  - **Do you sell** lenses?
    렌즈 파나요?

- **I'd like one that's …**
  ~ 편한 것이면 좋겠어요.
  - **I'd like one that's** easy to use.
    사용하기에 편한 것이면 좋겠어요.
  - **I'd like one that's** more compact.
    더 소형이면 좋겠어요.

- **It's made in …** ~ 제품입니다.
  - **It's made in** Germany.
    독일제입니다.
  - **It's made in** China.
    중국 제품입니다.

- **… come with …**
  ~ 에는 ~ 가 딸려있습니다.
  - The camera **comes with** a free camera bag.
    이 카메라에는 무료로 가방이 딸려있습니다.
  - This phone **comes with** a free headphone.
    이 전화기에는 무료 헤드폰이 딸려있습니다.

— STUDY TIP

'Thank you.'에 대한 다양한 대답:

You are welcome.
No problem.
No worries.
My pleasure.
Don't mention it.

대화를 들어보세요. 그런 다음 롤플레잉을 해보세요.

Kim ¹enters an ²electronics shop.
Kim은 전자제품 가게로 들어간다.

The ³salesclerk shows Kim some cameras.
판매원은 Kim에게 카메라들을 보여준다.

The salesclerk picks up a camera.
판매원은 카메라를 고른다.

Kim looks at the camera.
Kim은 카메라를 살펴본다.

Kim asks about the camera.
Kim은 카메라에 대해 물어본다.

Kim decides to buy the camera.
Kim은 카메라를 사기로 결정한다.

The salesclerk gives Kim a camera bag.
판매원은 Kim에게 카메라 가방을 건넨다.

Kim ⁸pays for the camera.
Kim은 카메라 비용을 지불한다.

MATCHING

올바른 영영 뜻을 B열에서 찾아 A열 옆에 쓰세요.

A

___ 1. electronics shop
___ 2. enter
___ 3. expensive
___ 4. free
___ 5. salesclerk

B

a. a worker who sells things in a store 점원
b. a store that sells electronics 전자제품 가게
c. to go inside 들어가다
d. costing a lot of money 비싼
e. given without payment 무료의

CONVERSATION

올바른 영어 표현으로 쓰고 말해보세요.

SECTION 3

Social Time

친구 만나기

Scan for Preview

DAY 11 At a Fast Food Restaurant
패스트푸드점에서

DAY 12 At the Movies
극장에서

DAY 13 Helping a Neighbor
이웃 돕기

DAY 14 At a Coffee Shop
커피숍에서

DAY 15 At the Museum
박물관에서

SOCIAL TIME
DAY 11

패스트푸드점에서
At a Fast Food Restaurant

— KEY VOCABULARY

order	(음식 또는 음료를) 주문하다
favorite	가장 좋아하는
cheese	치즈
chocolate milkshake	초콜릿 맛 밀크셰이크
place an order	~을 주문하다
pickle	피클
cashier	점원, 출납원
meal	식사, 끼니
ketchup	케첩
packet	꾸러미
tray	쟁반
delicious	맛있는
throw away	버리다
trash (syn. rubbish, litter)	쓰레기

— KEY EXPRESSIONS

- **What are you going to …?**
  무엇을 ~ 하실래요?
  - **What are you going to** order**?**
    무엇을 주문하실래요?
  - **What are you going to** get**?**
    무엇을 드실래요?
- **Could I have …?** ~ 을 주시겠어요?
  - **Could I have** some extra ketchup, please**?**
    케첩 좀 더 주시겠어요?
  - **Could I have** another mustard packet, please**?**
    머스타드 하나만 더 받을 수 있나요?
- **I'll get …** ~ 을 가져갈게요.
  - **I'll get** some straws.
    빨대 몇 개 가져갈게요.
  - **I'll get** some napkins.
    냅킨 좀 가져갈게요.
- **Are you finished with …?**
  ~ 는 다 드셨나요?
  - **Are you finished with** your shake**?**
    셰이크 다 마셨어요?
  - **Are you finished with** your sandwich**?**
    샌드위치 다 드셨나요?

— STUDY TIP

주문을 받을 때 사용할 수 있는 표현은:

May I take your order?
Can I take your order?
Are you ready to order?

대화를 들어보세요. 그런 다음 롤플레잉을 해보세요.

John and Mary talk about what to order.
John과 Mary는 뭘 주문할지에 대해 이야기를 나눈다.

John [5]places his order at the counter.
John은 카운터에서 주문한다.

Mary asks for a burger without pickles.
Mary는 피클을 빼고 버거만 주문한다.

The [7]cashier asks if it's for take-out.
점원이 가지고 갈 건지 아닌지 물어본다.

The cashier gives them their food.
점원이 그들에게 음식을 건넨다.

The cashier puts some more ketchup [10]packets on the [11]tray.
점원은 케첩 봉지를 식판에 추가한다.

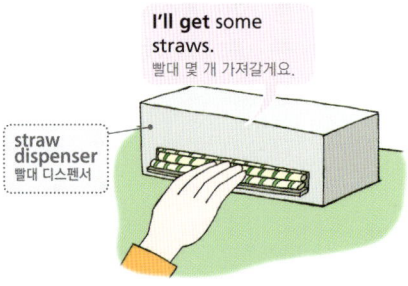

Mary gets some straws from the dispenser.
Mary는 빨대 몇 개를 디스펜서에서 꺼낸다.

After lunch, John [13]throws away the [14]trash.
점심식사 후, John은 쓰레기를 버린다.

MATCHING

올바른 영영 뜻을 B열에서 찾아 A열 옆에 쓰세요.

A	B
_____ 1. cashier	a. tasting very good 맛있는
_____ 2. chocolate milkshake	b. to put in the trash 버리다
_____ 3. delicious	c. a worker who takes payments from customers 점원
_____ 4. ketchup	d. a drink made by mixing chocolate, milk, and ice cream 초콜릿 맛 밀크세이크
_____ 5. throw away	e. a sauce made from tomatoes 케첩

CONVERSATION

올바른 영어 표현으로 쓰고 말해보세요.

SOCIAL TIME
DAY 12

극장에서
At the Movies

▬ KEY VOCABULARY

movie (syn. film)	영화
movie theater	영화관
ticket	티켓, 표
pass	전달하다, 건네다
popcorn	팝콘
snack	스낵, 간식
usher	안내원

▬ KEY EXPRESSIONS

- **Which … do you want to see?**
  어떤 ~ 을 볼래요?
  - **Which** movie **do you want to see?**
    어떤 영화 볼래요?
  - **Which** film **do you want to see?**
    어떤 영화 볼래요?

- **I heard … is good.** ~ 가 좋다던데요.
  - **I heard** Red Hearts **is good.**
    'Red Hearts'가 좋다던데요.
  - **I heard** Two Times to the Past **is good.**
    'Two Times to the Past'가 좋다던데요.

▬ STUDY TIP

영어의 감탄문에는 What으로 시작하는 감탄문과 How로 시작하는 감탄문이 있다.

What 감탄문 어순:
What +(a/an) + (형용사 + 명사) + (주어+동사)
What a great film (it is)!

How 감탄문 어순:
How + 형용사/부사 + (주어 + 동사)
How great the film is!

대화를 들어보세요. 그런 다음 롤플레잉을 해보세요.

Carlos and Julia walk into the ²movie theater.
Carlos와 Julia는 영화관으로 들어간다.

Carlos chooses tickets for the 8:00 show.
Carlos는 8시 티켓을 선택한다.

The cashier ⁴passes the tickets through the window.
점원은 티켓을 매표소 창으로 건넨다.

They get some ⁶snacks.
그들은 간식을 산다.

Carlos gives their tickets to the ⁷usher.
Carlos는 티켓을 안내원에게 건넨다.

The usher checks the tickets and gives back.
안내원은 티켓을 확인하고 돌려준다.

They find their seats.
그들은 자리를 찾는다.

Carlos and Julia watch the movie.
Carlos와 Julia는 영화를 본다.

MATCHING

올바른 영영 뜻을 B열에서 찾아 A열 옆에 쓰세요.

A	B
____ 1. movie	a. a place that shows movies 영화관
____ 2. movie theater	b. food you eat between meals 간식
____ 3. popcorn	c. a snack made from popped corn 팝콘
____ 4. snack	d. a piece of paper that shows you paid to enter 표
____ 5. ticket	e. a film shown in a cinema 영화

CONVERSATION

올바른 영어 표현으로 쓰고 말해보세요.

Which 1 _____ do you want to see?
어떤 영화 볼래요?

I heard *Red Hearts* is good.

Hi, two 2 _____ for *Red Hearts*, please.
'*Red Hearts*' 두 장 주세요.

OK. For 8:00 or 9:30?

8:00, please.

Here are your tickets. That will be $15, please.

Hi, one large 3 _____, and two 4 _____ colas, please.
안녕하세요. 팝콘 큰 것 하나와, 콜라 중간 것으로 2개 주세요.

That'll be $7.

Tickets, Please.

5 _____ you are.
여기 있습니다.

6 _____ four is on your left.
제 4 상영관은 왼쪽입니다.

Where are our 7 _____?
우리 자리가 어디죠?

They're over here.

What a great film!

This movie is terrible!

SOCIAL TIME
DAY 13

이웃 돕기
Helping a Neighbor

▬ KEY VOCABULARY

carry	운반하다, 나르다
grocery bag	장바구니
grandchild	손주
apartment	아파트
kitchen counter	부엌 조리대
garbage can	쓰레기통
garbage bag	쓰레기봉투

▬ KEY EXPRESSIONS

- **Let me ... for you.**
  제가 ~ 을 할게요.
  - **Let me** get the door **for you.**
    내가 문을 열게요.
  - **Let me** close the door **for you.**
    제가 문을 닫을게요.

- **Where should I put ...?**
  어디에 ~ 을 놓을까요?
  - **Where should I put** these?
    어디에 이것들을 놓을까요?
  - **Where should I put** my coat?
    제 코트를 어디 둘까요?

- **Would you mind ... ing?**
  ~ 해줄래요?
  - **Would you mind** taking out my trash?
    쓰레기를 밖으로 가져가 줄래요?
  - **Would you mind** mowing the loan for me?
    잔디를 깎아줄래요?

- **I'm so glad to ...**
  ~ 해서 기뻐요.
  - **I'm so glad to** have a neighbor like you.
    당신과 같은 이웃을 두어서 무척 기뻐요.
  - **I'm so glad to** have someone like you.
    당신과 같은 사람이 있어서 기뻐요.

▬ STUDY TIP

도움을 줄 때 사용할 수 있는 표현:

Can I help you?
How can I help you?
May I help you?
How may I help you?

대화를 들어보세요. 그런 다음 롤플레잉을 해보세요.

Peter offers to ¹carry ²grocery bags for Mrs. Price.
Peter는 Price부인에게 장바구니를 들어 주겠다고 나선다.

Peter carries the bags to the ⁴apartment.
Peter는 봉투들을 아파트까지 옮겨준다.

Mrs. Price opens her apartment door.
Price 부인은 자신의 아파트 문을 연다.

Mrs. Price tells Peter where to put the bags.
Price 부인은 Peter에게 봉투들을 어디에 놓을지 말한다.

Peter puts the bags on the kitchen counter.
Peter는 봉투들을 조리대에 놓는다.

Peter asks if he can still help.
Peter는 도와줄 일이 더 없는지 물어본다.

Mrs. Price points to the ⁶garbage can.
Price부인은 쓰레기통을 가리킨다.

Peter picks up the ⁷garbage bag.
Peter는 쓰레기봉투를 손에 든다.

MATCHING

올바른 영영 뜻을 B열에서 찾아 A열 옆에 쓰세요.

A	B
____ 1. apartment	a. the son or daughter of a person's child 손주
____ 2. carry	b. a bin to put trash in 쓰레기통
____ 3. garbage can	c. to pick something up and move it somewhere 운반하다
____ 4. grandchild	d. a set of rooms for living in that are part of a larger building 아파트
____ 5. grocery bag	e. a bag to carry food items in 장바구니

CONVERSATION

올바른 영어 표현으로 쓰고 말해보세요.

Hi, Mrs. Price. Can I 1 _____ you?
안녕하세요, Price 부인. 도와드릴까요?

Hi, Peter. That would be great. Thank you!

You sure got a lot of 2 _____!
정말 많이 사셨네요!

Well, my 3 _____ are visiting tomorrow.
네, 내일 손주들이 놀러 와요.

I see. That will be nice.

Yes. Let me get the 4 _____ for you.
그럼요. 내가 문을 열게요.

Where should I put these?

Please put them on the 5 _____ counter.
부엌 조리대에 놔주세요.

Right here?

Yes. That's 6 _____. Thank you so much!
그래요. 좋아요. 너무 고마워요.

Is there anything else I can do for you?

Would you mind taking out my 7 _____?
쓰레기를 밖으로 가져가 줄래요?

Of course not.

I'm so glad to have a 8 _____ like you, Peter!
자네와 같은 이웃이 있어서 무척 기뻐요, Peter!

SOCIAL TIME
DAY 14

커피숍에서
At a Coffee Shop

━ KEY VOCABULARY

coffee	커피, 커피 한 잔
decaffeinated coffee	카페인이 없는 커피
low-fat	저지방의
cappuccino	카푸치노
cream	크림
sugar	설탕
exhibit	전시, 전시품
art museum	미술관
give a call	전화하다
pour	붓다, 따르다
stir	젓다, 섞다

━ KEY EXPRESSIONS

- **Welcome to …** ~ 에 오신 것을 환영합니다.
  - **Welcome to** Moonbucks.
    문벅에 오신 것을 환영합니다.
  - **Welcome to** Walworth's.
    왈워스에 오신 것을 환영합니다.

- **I'd like …** ~ 로 할게요.
  - **I'd like** a low-fat cappuccino.
    저지방 카푸치노로 할게요.
  - **I'd like** a hot vanilla latte.
    따듯한 바닐라 라테로 할게요.

- **You can get … over there.**
  저쪽에서 ~ 를 받아 가세요.
  - **You can get** your drinks **over there.**
    저쪽에서 주문하신 음료를 받아 가세요.
  - **You can get** your membership card **over there.**
    저쪽에서 회원 카드를 받아 가세요.

- **Can you get … for me?**
  저에게 ~ 를 주실래요?
  - **Can you get** some cream and sugar **for me?**
    저에게 설탕과 크림을 좀 주실래요?
  - **Can you get** some napkins **for me?**
    저에게 냅킨을 좀 주실래요?

━ STUDY TIP

다양한 커피 종류:

Espresso / Latte / Vienna Coffee / Mocha

대화를 들어보세요. 그런 다음 롤플레잉을 해보세요.

Hi, **welcome to** Moonbucks. How can I help you?
안녕하세요. 문벅입니다. 무엇을 도와드릴까요?

I'll have a large ¹coffee.
라지 커피로 하나 주세요.

mug 손잡이가 달린 찻잔

Mary and Kim go to the coffee shop counter.
Mary와 Kim은 커피숍 카운터로 간다.

Regular or decaf, ma'am?
레귤러, 아니면 카페인이 없는 거로요, 부인?

Decaf, please.
카페인 없는 거로요.

Mary asks for ²decaffeinated coffee.
Mary는 카페인이 없는 커피를 주문한다.

I'd like a ³low-fat ⁴cappuccino, please.
저는 저지방 카푸치노로 할게요.

OK. Would you like anything else?
네, 다른 것은 필요하지 않으세요?

No, thanks.
아니요, 고맙습니다.

Kim places her order.
Kim이 마실 것을 주문한다.

A large decaf and a low-fat cappuccino. Here you go.
카페인이 없는 라지 커피 한 잔과 저지방 카푸치노 한 잔, 여기 나왔습니다.

Thanks.
고마워요.

Mary gets their coffee.
Mary가 커피를 받는다.

That will be $6.50, please. **You can get** your drinks **over there.**
6.5달러예요. 저쪽에서 주문하신 음료를 받아 가세요.

The cashier points to the pick-up counter.
점원이 픽업 카운터를 가리킨다.

Can you get some ⁵cream and ⁶sugar **for me?**
크림과 설탕 좀 집어주시겠어요?

Sure.
그러지요.

Kim picks up some sugar packets and cream for Mary.
Kim은 Mary에게 설탕 봉지와 크림을 집어준다.

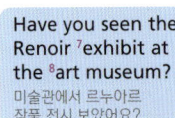

Have you seen the Renoir ⁷exhibit at the ⁸art museum?
미술관에서 르누아르 작품 전시 보았어요?

Yes. I went last weekend. It was wonderful!
네, 지난 주말에 갔었는데, 훌륭했어요.

They sit down at a table by the window.
그들은 창가에 자리를 잡는다.

Great idea. I'll ⁹give him a call.
좋은 생각이에요. 전화해야겠어요.

Peter wants to see it, too. You should go together.
Peter도 보고 싶어 해요. 꼭 같이 가보세요.

stir stick 휘젓는 막대

Mary ¹⁰pours some cream into her coffee and ¹¹stirs it.
Mary는 자신의 커피에 크림을 넣고 젓는다.

MATCHING

올바른 영영 뜻을 B열에서 찾아 A열 옆에 쓰세요.

A	B
____ 1. cream	a. coffee that does not have caffeine in it 카페인이 없는 커피
____ 2. decaffeinated coffee	b. a white powder that makes food sweet 설탕
____ 3. exhibit	c. the thick, fatty part of milk 크림
____ 4. pour	d. a collection of art in a show 전시
____ 5. sugar	e. to drop liquid from something 붓다

CONVERSATION

올바른 영어 표현으로 쓰고 말해보세요.

SOCIAL TIME
DAY 15
박물관에서
At the Museum

KEY VOCABULARY

request (syn. ask for)	요청하다
taxi	택시
reach for	손을 뻗다
fair	공평한
agree	동의하다, 의견이 일치하다
share	나누다, 공유하다
cost	비용
guided tour	가이드 투어
take a picture	사진을 찍다, 촬영하다
sculpture	조각, 조소

KEY EXPRESSIONS

- **That sounds …** ~ 하네요.
  - **That sounds** fair.
    공평하네요.
  - **That sounds** fine.
    좋네요.

- **Are there …?** ~ 가 있나요?
  - **Are there** guided tours?
    가이드의 안내가 있나요?
  - **Are there** audio tours?
    오디오 투어가 있나요?

- **You can't …** ~ 하시면 안 됩니다.
  - **You can't** take pictures here.
    여기서 사진 찍으시면 안 됩니다.
  - **You can't** record audio here.
    여기서 녹음하시면 안 됩니다.

- **What was your favorite …?**
  ~ 가 가장 마음에 들었어요?
  - **What was your favorite** part?
    어느 부분이 가장 마음에 들었어요?
  - **What was your favorite** painting in the exhibition?
    이 전시에서 가장 마음에 든 그림이 무엇이에요?

STUDY TIP

우리나라에서는 각자 돈을 나눠서 내자는 뜻으로 Dutch pay(더치페이) 하자고 흔히 얘기하는데, 이는 우리나라식으로 변형되어 잘못 쓰이는 표현이고 'Let's go dutch.' 가 영어식 표현이다. 비슷한 표현으로는 'Let's split the bill.' 이 있다.

대화를 들어보세요. 그런 다음 롤플레잉을 해보세요.

Hi. Two, please.
안녕하세요. 두 장 부탁합니다.

That's $16.
16달러입니다.

Peter ¹requests two tickets.
Peter는 두 장의 티켓을 요청한다.

Let me get this. You paid for the ²taxi.
이건 제가 낼게요. 당신이 택시비 내셨으니까.

It's no trouble, really.
괜찮아요. 정말로.

Kim ³reaches for her purse.
Kim은 지갑으로 손을 가져간다.

Well, let's go Dutch, then.
그럼, 각자 부담해요.

OK. That sounds ⁴fair.
좋아요. 공평하네요.

Are there ⁸guided tours?
가이드의 안내가 있나요?

Yes. The next one will start in a few minutes.
네. 다음 안내는 몇 분 후에 시작됩니다.

They ⁵agree to ⁶share the ⁷cost of the tickets.
그들은 티켓 비용을 나누어 내는 데 동의한다.

The ticket seller points to the schedule.
티켓 판매원이 스케줄을 가리킨다.

This is one of Renoir's first works…
이건 르누아르의 초기 작품 중 하나로…

Wow! It's beautiful
와! 아름답다!

Yes, amazing!
네, 정말 훌륭해요!

Excuse me, ma'am. You can't ⁹take pictures here.
실례합니다. 여기서는 사진 촬영이 금지되어 있습니다.

Oh! I'm sorry.
오! 미안합니다.

security guard
안전요원

Kim and Peter go on the tour.
Kim과 Peter는 관람을 시작한다.

Kim tries to take a picture.
Kim은 사진을 촬영하려 한다.

When was this made?
이건 언제 작품인가요?

It was made in 1845.
그건 1845년에 만들어졌어요.

What was your favorite part?
어느 부분이 가장 마음에 들었어요?

I liked the sculpture best.
조각품이 가장 좋았어요.

Peter asks a question about the ¹⁰sculpture.
Peter는 조각품에 대해 질문한다.

Kim and Peter talk about what they have seen.
Kim과 Peter는 자신들이 본 것에 대해 이야기를 나눈다.

MATCHING

올바른 영영 뜻을 B열에서 찾아 A열 옆에 쓰세요.

A	B
___ 1. agree	a. how much you pay for something 비용
___ 2. cost	b. to move your hand toward something 손을 뻗다
___ 3. reach for	c. an artwork made of clay or stone 조각
___ 4. request	d. to ask for something 요청하다
___ 5. sculpture	e. to have the same opinion 동의하다

CONVERSATION

올바른 영어 표현으로 쓰고 말해보세요.

- Hi. Two, please.
- That's $16.
- Let me get this. You paid for the 1 _____. 이건 제가 낼게요. 당신이 택시비 내셨으니까.
- It's no 2 _____, really. 괜찮아요. 정말로.
- Well, let's go Dutch, then.
- OK. That sounds 3 _____. 좋아요. 공평하네요.
- Are there 4 _____ tours? 가이드의 안내가 있나요?
- Yes. The next one will start in a few minutes.
- Wow! It's beautiful!
- This is one of Renoir's first works...
- Yes, 5 _____! 네, 정말 훌륭해요!
- Excuse me, ma'am. You can't take 6 _____ here. 실례합니다. 여기서는 사진 촬영이 금지되어 있습니다.
- Oh! I'm sorry.
- When was this made?
- It was 7 _____ in 1845. 그건 1845년에 만들어졌어요.
- What was your 8 _____ part? 어느 부분이 가장 마음에 들었어요?
- I liked the sculpture best.

SECTION 3 SOCIAL TIME 41

DAY 16 Taking a Taxi
택시 타기

DAY 17 In the Library
도서관에서

DAY 18 Taking a Bus
버스 타기

DAY 19 Getting Gas
주유하기

DAY 20 Asking for Directions
길 묻기

AROUND THE TOWN

DAY 16

택시 타기
Taking a Taxi

▬ KEY VOCABULARY

cab (syn. taxi)	택시
hail a taxi	택시를 부르다
direction	방향
near	가까운
turn on	~을 켜다
meter	미터기
chat	대화하다, 담소를 나누다
in front of	~의 앞쪽에
concert hall	콘서트홀
fare (syn. charge, price)	(버스, 택시, 기차 등의) 차비, 요금

▬ KEY EXPRESSIONS

- **Do you want to take …?**
  ~를 타실래요?
  - **Do you want to take** a taxi or the bus?
    택시를 타실래요, 아니면 버스를 타실래요?
  - **Do you want to take** the subway?
    지하철을 타실래요?

- **Let's take …** ~을 탑시다.
  - **Let's take** a cab.
    택시 탑시다.
  - **Let's take** the bus.
    버스 탑시다.

- **We are going to …** ~로 갑시다.
  - **We are going to** the Austin Concert Hall on Dover Street.
    도버가 오스틴 콘서트홀로 갑시다.
  - **We are going to** Madison Square Garden.
    매디슨 스퀘어 가든으로 갑시다.

▬ STUDY TIP

교통체증과 관련된 영어 표현:

1. 교통체증이 심각할 때
The traffic is terrible.
The traffic is bad.
The traffic is heavy.
The traffic is crawling.
There is a lot of traffic.
The traffic was bumper to bumper.

2. 차가 막히지 않을 때
The traffic is light.
There is no traffic.
There is little traffic.
The traffic is good.
It is not congested.

대화를 들어보세요. 그런 다음 롤플레잉을 해보세요.

Peter and Kim decide to take a taxi.
Peter와 Kim은 택시를 타기로 결정한다.

Peter [2]hails a taxi.
Peter는 택시를 부른다.

Peter opens the door for Kim.
Peter는 Kim을 위해 문을 연다.

Peter gives the driver [3]directions.
Peter는 운전사에게 방향을 얘기한다.

The taxi driver [5]turns on the [6]meter.
택시 운전사는 미터기를 켠다.

They [7]chat with the driver.
그들은 운전사와 가벼운 얘기를 나눈다.

The taxi stops [8]in front of the [9]concert hall.
택시는 콘서트홀 앞에 선다.

Peter pays the [10]fare.
Peter는 요금을 지불한다.

MATCHING

올바른 영영 뜻을 B열에서 찾아 A열 옆에 쓰세요.

A	B
___ 1. chat	a. to call a taxi 택시를 부르다
___ 2. concert hall	b. to talk in a friendly way 대화하다
___ 3. fare	c. close to 가까운
___ 4. hail a taxi	d. a building that holds musical events 콘서트홀
___ 5. near	e. the cost of a ride 요금

CONVERSATION

올바른 영어 표현으로 쓰고 말해보세요.

Do you 1 _____ take a taxi or the bus?
택시를 타실래요, 아니면 버스를 타실래요?

Let's 2 _____.
It's faster.
택시 탑시다. 그게 빠르니까.

TAXI!

After you.

Thanks.

We're 3 _____ the Austin Concert Hall on Dover Street.
도버가 오스틴 콘서트홀로 갑시다.

Where to, sir?

Is that near Victoria Park?

Yes. That's right.

The traffic is 4 _____ today.
오늘은 교통량이 많지 않네요.

Yes. It's very light.

Here 5 _____.
That'll be $6.50 please.
도착했습니다. 요금은 6달러 50센트네요.

Thank you. Have 7 _____!
고맙습니다. 좋은 하루 되세요!

Here you go.
Keep 6 _____.
여기 있습니다. 잔돈은 가지세요.

AROUND THE TOWN
DAY 17
도서관에서
In the Library

▬ KEY VOCABULARY

mystery	미스터리, 추리소설
library	도서관
search	검색하다, 찾다
author (syn. writer)	저자, 작가
call number	등록번호, 청구번호
thriller	스릴러물
shelf	선반, 책꽂이, 칸
famous (syn. well-known)	유명한
thief (syn. robber)	도둑, 절도범
century	세기 (100년의 기간)
copy	한 부
recommend	추천하다, 권하다
return	반납하다
check out	(책을) 대출하다

▬ KEY EXPRESSIONS

- **I love …** 저는 ~ 를 좋아해요.
  - **I love** mysteries.
    저는 추리소설을 좋아해요.
  - **I love** thrillers.
    저는 스릴러를 좋아해요.

- **It's called …** ~ 라 불립니다. / ~ 입니다.
  - **It's called** *The Diamond Thief*.
    '*The Diamond Thief*' 라는 책입니다.
  - **It's called** *Blessings at Midnight*.
    '*Blessings at Midnight*' 입니다.

- **Who is your favorite …?**
  가장 좋아하는 ~ 가 누군가요?
  - **Who is your favorite** author?
    가장 좋아하는 작가가 누군가요?
  - **Who is your favorite** writer?
    가장 좋아하는 작가가 누군가요?

- **What's … about?**
  ~ 은 무슨 내용이에요?
  - **What's** it **about**?
    이것은 무슨 내용이에요?
  - **What's** this book **about**?
    이 책은 무슨 내용이에요?

▬ STUDY TIP

다양한 책 종류:

autobiography 자서전
fable 우화
fairy tale 동화
fantasy 판타지
historical fiction 역사 소설
legend 전설
myth 신화
poetry 시
tall tale 믿기 어려운 이야기, 과장된 이야기
traditional literature 전통 문학

대화를 들어보세요. 그런 다음 롤플레잉을 해보세요.

Julia and Carlos walk into the ²library.
Julia와 Carlos는 도서관으로 들어간다.

Julia ³searches for a book.
Julia는 책을 찾는다.

Julia writes down the book's ⁵call number.
Julia는 책의 등록번호를 적는다.

They walk down the aisle.
그들은 통로를 따라 걸어간다.

aisle 통로

Julia pulls the book off the ⁷shelf.
Julia는 책꽂이에서 그 책을 꺼낸다.

Julia reads the jacket of the book...
Julia는 책 표지의 글을 읽는다.

...and ¹²recommends the book to Carlos.
그리고 그 책을 Carlos에게 권한다.

They ¹⁴check out their books.
그들은 책을 대출한다.

librarian 사서

MATCHING

올바른 영영 뜻을 B열에서 찾아 A열 옆에 쓰세요.

A	B
___ 1. author	a. one hundred years 세기
___ 2. century	b. to bring something back 반납하다
___ 3. return	c. someone who steals something 도둑
___ 4. search	d. to look for something 검색하다
___ 5. thief	e. someone who writes a book 저자

CONVERSATION

올바른 영어 표현으로 쓰고 말해보세요.

What 1 _____ of books do you like?
어떤 종류의 책을 좋아하세요?

I love mysteries.

It's called The Diamond Thief.

What book are you 2 _____?
무슨 책을 찾아요?

Who's the author?

Glen Hill. OK. It's number H-237.

What about you? Who is your 3 _____?
당신은요? 좋아하는 작가가 누군가요?

Tom Clancy. I love thrillers.

Here it is!

What's it about?

It's about a 4 _____ in Paris in the 18th century.
이건 18세기 파리의 어느 유명한 도둑에 관한 책이에요.

Sounds 5 _____.
재미있겠네요.

There's 6 _____. Let's read it together!
한 권 더 있는데, 같이 읽죠!

Good idea.

When should we return these?

In 7 _____.
2주 이내예요.

AROUND THE TOWN

DAY 18

버스 타기
Taking a Bus

▬ KEY VOCABULARY

often	자주, 보통
bench	벤치
stop (syn. station)	정류장
far	멀리, 떨어져
mall	쇼핑몰, 대형 쇼핑센터
seat	자리, 좌석
ring	벨을 누르다, 신호를 올리다

▬ KEY EXPRESSIONS

- **Which bus goes to ...?**
  ~에 가려면 어떤 버스를 타야죠?
  - **Which bus goes to** Regent Mall**?**
    리젠트 몰에 가려면 어느 버스를 타야죠?
  - **Which bus goes to** Center City**?**
    센터 시티에 가려면 어느 버스를 타야죠?

- **How often does ...** (교통수단) **come?**
  ~가 몇 분 간격으로 다니죠?
  - **How often does** it **come?**
    몇 분 간격으로 다니죠?
  - **How often does** the bus **come?**
    그 버스는 몇 분 간격으로 다니죠?

- **It comes every ...** ~ 마다 옵니다.
  - **It comes every** ten minutes.
    10분마다 옵니다.
  - **It comes every** half hour.
    30분마다 옵니다.

- **... get on ...** ~은 ~에 탄다.
  - Kim **gets on** the bus.
    Kim은 버스에 탄다.
  - Jenny **gets on** the train.
    Jenny는 열차에 탄다.

▬ STUDY TIP

offer A to B
A를 B에게 제공하다.

Kim offers <u>her seat</u> to <u>another person</u>.
Kim은 다른 사람에게 자리를 양보한다.

The hotel offers <u>free breakfast</u> to <u>all customers</u>.
그 호텔은 모든 고객에게 무료 조식을 제공한다.

대화를 들어보세요. 그런 다음 롤플레잉을 해보세요.

Kim asks a person about the bus schedule.
Kim은 버스 스케줄에 대해 어떤 사람에게 물어본다.

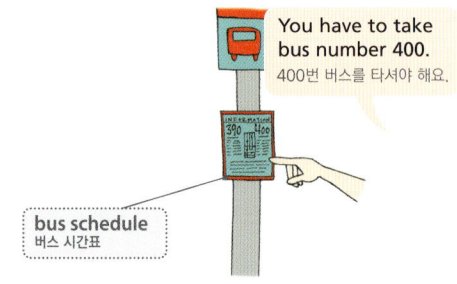

The person tells Kim which bus to take.
그 사람은 Kim에게 어느 버스를 타야 할지 알려준다.

Kim sits down on the ²bench.
Kim은 벤치에 앉는다.

Kim **gets on** the bus.
Kim은 버스에 오른다.

The bus driver tells Kim the fare.
버스 운전사는 Kim에게 요금을 얘기한다.

Kim asks how ⁴far the ⁵mall is.
Kim은 그 쇼핑센터가 얼마나 먼지 물어본다.

Kim offers her seat to another person.
Kim은 다른 사람에게 자리를 양보한다.

Kim ⁷rings for her stop.
Kim은 내릴 정거장의 신호를 울린다.

MATCHING

올바른 영영 뜻을 B열에서 찾아 A열 옆에 쓰세요.

A	B
___ 1. bench	a. not close by 멀리
___ 2. far	b. a long seat, usually for two or more people 벤치
___ 3. mall	c. a place to sit down; a chair 자리
___ 4. often	d. a large shopping area with many stores 쇼핑몰
___ 5. seat	e. happening frequently 자주

CONVERSATION

올바른 영어 표현으로 쓰고 말해보세요.

Excuse me, which bus goes to Regent Mall?

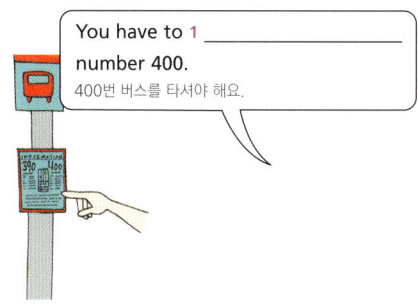
You have to 1 _____ number 400.
400번 버스를 타셔야 해요.

2 _____ does it come?
몇 분 간격으로 다니죠?

It comes every 10 minutes.

Here's the bus. Thanks for 3 _____.
버스가 오네요. 도와주셔서 고마워요.

No problem!

How much is it?

That's $1.80.

4 _____ to Regent Mall?
리젠트 몰까지는 몇 정거장이죠?

About 11 stops, ma'am.

Ma'am? You can 5 _____.
부인? 여기 앉으세요.

Oh, thank you. You're so 6 _____!
오 고마워요. 매우 친절하시군요.

Next stop, Regent Mall!

DAY 19

AROUND THE TOWN

주유하기
Getting Gas

KEY VOCABULARY

gas station	주유소
up ahead	앞쪽에, 전방에
save money	돈을 절약하다
lane	차선
cover	뚜껑, 덮개
unleaded (ant. leaded)	무연의
unscrew	열다
worth	~어치, 만큼
pump	펌프
lever	레버
squeeze	눌러 잡다, 꽉 쥐다

KEY EXPRESSIONS

- **I should get …** ~ 를 해야겠어요.
  - **I should get** some gas.
    기름 좀 넣어야겠어요.
  - **I should get** some rest.
    좀 쉬어야겠어요.

- **It saves …** ~ 이 절약됩니다.
  - **It saves** money.
    돈이 절약됩니다.
  - **It saves** time.
    시간이 절약됩니다.

- **Just …** 그냥 ~ 로요.
  - **Just** regular unleaded.
    그냥 보통 무연 휘발유로요.
  - **Just** premium, please.
    그냥 고급 휘발유로요.

STUDY TIP

주유소에서 자주 쓰이는 단어들:

automatic car wash 자동 세차
diesel 경유
fueling 주유
premium unleaded 고급 휘발유
unleaded 무연 휘발유

대화를 들어보세요. 그런 다음 롤플레잉을 해보세요.

Julia points down the road.
Julia는 길을 가리킨다.

They pull into the self-serve [4]lane at the station.
그들은 셀프서비스 선으로 들어선다.

Julia gets out of the car.
Julia는 차에서 내린다.

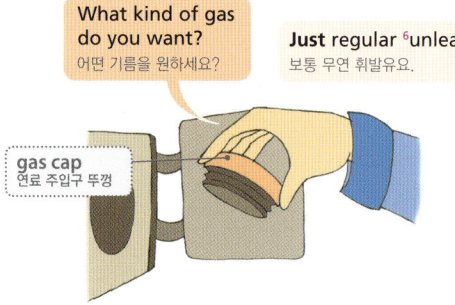

Julia [7]unscrews the gas cap.
Julia는 주유구 뚜껑을 돌려 연다.

Julia takes the nozzle off the [9]pump and lifts the [10]lever.
Julia는 분사기를 펌프에서 빼고 레버를 올린다.

Julia inserts the nozzle and [11]squeezes the handle.
Julia는 분사기를 넣고 핸들을 꽉 쥔다.

Julia puts her card in the slot and pays for the gas.
Julia는 카드를 기계에 삽입하고 돈을 지불한다.

Julia and Carlos get back in the car.
Julia와 Carlos는 차로 돌아간다.

MATCHING

올바른 영영 뜻을 B열에서 찾아 A열 옆에 쓰세요.

A	B
_____ 1. gas station	a. a place that sells gas 주유소
_____ 2. lane	b. to press something firmly 꽉 쥐다
_____ 3. pump	c. a tool that pushes gas into a car's tank 펌프
_____ 4. save money	d. a part of a road that is for a single line of cars 차선
_____ 5. squeeze	e. to not spend your money 돈을 절약하다

CONVERSATION

올바른 영어 표현으로 쓰고 말해보세요.

There's a 1 _____ up ahead.
앞쪽에 주유소가 있네요.

Really? I should 2 _____.
그래요? 기름 좀 넣어야겠어요.

Full-serve or self-serve?

I always use self-serve. It 3 _____.
저는 항상 셀프를 이용해요. 돈이 절약되거든요.

OK, thanks.

I'll do it. Please 4 _____.
제가 할게요. 주유구 덮개를 여세요.

What 5 _____ do you want?
어떤 기름을 원하세요?

Just regular unleaded.

Let's get $20. 6 _____.
20달러 정도만 넣읍시다.

How much do you want?

I need the 7 _____. Do you want anything from inside?
화장실 좀 다녀와야겠어요. 안에서 필요한 거 있어요?

No thank you.

8 _____, let's go.
다 됐어요. 갑시다.

DAY 20 — AROUND THE TOWN
길 묻기 — Asking for Directions

KEY VOCABULARY

anyway	어쨌든, 그건 그렇고
pardon me	실례합니다
second	두 번째의
stoplight	정지신호
confirm	확인하다, 확정하다

KEY EXPRESSIONS

- **How can we get to …?**
  ~ 에 어떻게 가죠?
  - **How can we get to** the Blue Moon jazz club**?**
    블루문 재즈 클럽에 어떻게 가죠?
  - **How can we get to** the Meridian Palace**?**
    메리디안 팰리스에 어떻게 가죠?

- **Do you know where … is?**
  ~ 가 어딘지 아세요?
  - **Do you know where** it **is?**
    여기가 어딘지 아세요?
  - **Do you know where** the mall **is?**
    몰이 어딘지 아세요?

- **Turn …** (방향) ~ 로 돌아서 ~
  - **Turn** left onto Apollo Ave. and go about four blocks.
    아폴로가 쪽으로 좌회전한 후 네 블록쯤 가세요.
  - **Turn** right at the light up ahead and go straight for four miles.
    앞에 있는 신호등에서 우회전한 후 4마일 직진하세요.

- **It's on your …** 당신의 ~ 쪽이에요.
  - **It's on your** right.
    당신의 오른쪽이에요.
  - **It's on your** left.
    당신의 왼쪽이에요.

STUDY TIP

길을 나타내는 표현:

avenue (Ave.) 시내의 도로, 거리, 가
남-북 간을 잇는 (세로) 시가지 도로

road (Rd.) 도로, 포장된 길
두 지점을 연결하는 모든 종류의 길

street (St.) 시내의 도로, 거리, 가
동-서 간을 잇는 (가로) 시가지 도로

일반적으로 street는 조금 촘촘하게, avenue는 큰 하나의 블록으로 구역을 나누어 도로를 만든다.

대화를 들어보세요. 그런 다음 롤플레잉을 해보세요.

I don't know where it is.
어딘지 모르겠어요.

Let's stop and ask for directions.
차를 세워 길을 물어보죠.

Julia and Carlos are lost.
Julia와 Carlos는 길을 잃었다.

Excuse me, sir. **How can we get to** the Blue Moon jazz club?
실례합니다, 선생님. 블루문 재즈 클럽에 어떻게 가죠?

street light
가로등

Julia asks for directions.
Julia는 길을 묻는다.

I'm sorry. I have no idea.
미안하지만, 모르겠는데요.

Thanks [1]anyway.
어쨌든 고맙습니다.

The man cannot help them.
남자는 이들을 도와줄 수 없다.

[2]Pardon me, ma'am. We're looking for the Blue Moon jazz club. **Do you know** where it **is**?
실례합니다만, 블루문 재즈 클럽을 찾고 있는데요. 어딘지 아세요?

Julia asks another person.
Julia는 다른 사람에게 물어본다.

Sure. Drive down this road to the [3]second [4]stoplight.
네, 이 길을 따라 두 번째 신호등까지 가세요.

The woman points down the road.
여자는 길을 가리킨다.

OK. Second stoplight.
아, 두 번째 신호등이요.

Yes. Then **turn** left onto Apollo Ave. and go about four blocks. **It's on your** right.
맞아요. 아폴로가 쪽으로 좌회전한 후 네 블록쯤 가면 오른쪽에 있어요.

The woman gives them more directions.
여자는 상세히 안내한다.

Take a left on Apollo, four blocks down on the right?
아폴로가에서 좌회전하고 네 블록쯤 가면 오른쪽에 있어요?

Yes. It's next to the Mirage Theater.
네, 미라즈 영화관 옆이에요.

Julia [5]confirms the directions.
Julia는 길을 확인한다.

No problem. Have fun!
천만에요. 좋은 시간 되세요.

Thanks a lot!
고맙습니다!

Julia thanks the woman for her help.
Julia는 여자에게 고맙다는 인사를 한다.

MATCHING

올바른 영영 뜻을 B열에서 찾아 A열 옆에 쓰세요.

A	B
____ 1. anyway	a. to say sorry for interrupting someone 실례합니다
____ 2. confirm	b. lights that tell drivers to go, slow down, and stop 정지신호
____ 3. pardon me	c. in any case; at least 어쨌든
____ 4. second	d. after first and before third 두 번째의
____ 5. stoplight	e. to make sure information is correct 확인하다

CONVERSATION

올바른 영어 표현으로 쓰고 말해보세요.

I don't know where it is.

Let's stop and 1 _____.
차를 세워 길을 물어보죠.

Excuse me, sir. 2 _____ get to the Blue Moon jazz club?
실례합니다, 선생님.
블루문 재즈 클럽에 어떻게 가죠?

I'm sorry. I have 3 _____.
미안하지만, 모르겠는데요.

Thanks anyway.

4 _____, ma'am. We're looking for the Blue Moon jazz club. Do you know where it is?
실례합니다만, 블루문 재즈 클럽을 찾고 있는데요. 어딘지 아세요?

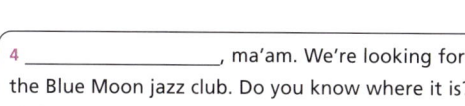

Sure. Drive 5 _____ to the second stoplight.
네. 이 길을 따라 두 번째 신호등까지 가세요.

OK. Second stoplight.

Yes. Then turn left onto Apollo Ave. and go about four blocks. It's 6 _____.
맞아요. 아폴로가 쪽으로 좌회전한 후 네 블록쯤 가면 오른쪽에 있어요.

Take a left on Apollo, 7 _____ down on the right?
아폴로가에서 좌회전하고
네 블록쯤 가면 오른쪽에 있어요?

Yes. It's next to the Mirage Theater.

No problem. 8 _____!
천만에요. 좋은 시간 되세요.

Thanks a lot!

SECTION 4 AROUND THE TOWN

SECTION 5

Restaurant

레스토랑에서 식사하기

DAY 21 Arriving at the Restaurant
식당에서

DAY 22 Ordering Drinks and an Appetizer
음료와 애피타이저 주문

DAY 23 The Waiter Returns
웨이터가 돌아오다

DAY 24 The Food Arrives
음식이 도착하다

DAY 25 A Lovely Meal
맛있는 식사

RESTAURANT
DAY 21

식당에서
Arriving at the Restaurant

─ KEY VOCABULARY

reservation (syn. booking)	예약
host	안내자, 운영자
follow	(~의 뒤를) 따라가다
satisfy	만족하다
different	다른
today's special	오늘의 특선요리
sea bass	바다 농어
pasta	파스타
waiter	웨이터

─ KEY EXPRESSIONS

- **We have a reservation for …**
  ~ 로 예약했습니다.
  - **We have a reservation for** 7:30.
    7시 30분으로 예약했습니다.
  - **We have a reservation for** 9 o'clock.
    9시로 예약했습니다.

- **Will … be all right?**
  ~ 괜찮으세요?
  - **Will** this **be all right?**
    여기 괜찮으세요?
  - **Will** sparkling water **be all right?**
    탄산수 괜찮으세요?

- **Do you have … next to …?**
  ~ 옆에 ~ 가 있나요?
  - **Do you have** a table **next to** the window?
    창가 옆 테이블이 있나요?
  - **Do you have** a seat **next to** the door?
    문 옆에 자리가 있나요?

- **… will be with you …**
  ~ 가 당신을 모실 겁니다.
  - Your waiter **will be with you** shortly.
    웨이터가 여러분을 곧 모실 겁니다.
  - Your waiter **will be with you** in a couple of minutes.
    웨이터가 여러분을 잠시 후에 모실 겁니다.

─ STUDY TIP

예약했음을 이야기할 때 사용할 수 있는 표현:
We booked a table for two for 7:30.
7시 30분에 두 명 테이블을 예약했어요.
Our reservation is under the name of James at 7:30 for two people.
James 이름으로 7시 30분에 두 명 예약했어요.

대화를 들어보세요. 그런 다음 롤플레잉을 해보세요.

Good evening.
안녕하세요.

John and Mary Smith. **We have a ¹reservation for** 7:30.
John Smith와 Mary Smith입니다. 7시 30분으로 예약했는데요.

Yes… Mr. and Mrs. Smith. I have your reservation here.
네. Smith 부부, 여기 예약이 되어있네요.

John checks in with the ²host.
John은 안내자에게 예약 확인을 요청한다.

The host checks the reservation list.
안내자는 예약 목록을 확인한다.

Please ³follow me.
저를 따라오십시오.

All right.
네.

Will this **be all right?**
여기 괜찮으세요?

tablecloth
식탁보

The couple follows the host to the table.
부부는 안내자를 따라 테이블로 간다.

The host asks the couple if they are ⁴satisfied.
안내자는 부부가 자리에 만족하는지 물어본다.

Do you have a table **next to** the window?
창가 테이블은 없나요?

How is this?
여기는 어떠신가요?

Much better, thank you.
훨씬 좋군요. 고맙습니다.

John asks for a ⁵different table.
John은 다른 테이블을 요청한다.

The host takes them to another table.
안내자는 그들을 다른 테이블로 안내한다.

⁶Today's special is ⁷sea bass and ⁸pasta for $10.99.
오늘의 특선 요리는 바다 농어와 파스타로 10달러 99센트입니다.

Your ⁹waiter will be with you shortly.
웨이터가 여러분을 곧 모실 겁니다.

Thank you.
고맙습니다.

The host gives them menus and then tells them about the specials.
안내자는 메뉴판을 건네고 특별 요리에 대해 이야기한다.

The host leaves.
안내자는 테이블을 떠난다.

MATCHING

올바른 영영 뜻을 B열에서 찾아 A열 옆에 쓰세요.

A
_____ 1. different
_____ 2. follow
_____ 3. pasta
_____ 4. sea bass
_____ 5. waiter

B
a. to move behind and go where someone goes (~의 뒤를) 따라가다
b. a restaurant worker who serves food 웨이터
c. not the same 다른
d. a fish that lives in the sea 농어
e. a food made from noodles and sauce 파스타

CONVERSATION

올바른 영어 표현으로 쓰고 말해보세요.

Good evening.

John and Mary Smith. We 1 _____ for 7:30.
John Smith와 Mary Smith입니다. 7시 30분으로 예약했는데요.

Yes... Mr. and Mrs. Smith. I 2 _____ here.
네. Smith 부부, 여기 예약이 되어있네요.

Please 3 _____.
저를 따라오십시오.

All right.

Will this be 4 _____?
여기 괜찮으세요?

Do you have a table 5 _____ the window?
창가 테이블은 없나요?

How is this?

Much better, thank you.

6 _____ is sea bass and pasta for $10.99.
오늘의 특선 요리는 바다 농어와 파스타로 10달러 99센트입니다.

Your waiter will be 7 _____ shortly.
웨이터가 여러분을 곧 모실 겁니다.

Thank you.

RESTAURANT
DAY 22

음료와 애피타이저 주문
Ordering Drinks and an Appetizer

▬ KEY VOCABULARY

couple	커플, 부부
lemonade	레모네이드
appetizer	전채, 애피타이저
honey	(호칭으로) 여보
calamari	칼라마리 (식용 오징어)
decide (syn. choose)	결정하다

▬ KEY EXPRESSIONS

- **Everything looks …**
  모든 것이 ~ 해 보이네요.
  - **Everything looks** delicious!
    모든 것이 맛있어 보이네요!
  - **Everything looks** wonderful!
    모든 것이 훌륭해 보이네요!

- **Can I get you anything to …?**
  ~ 할 것 좀 가져다드릴까요?
  - **Can I get you anything to** drink?
    마실 것 좀 드릴까요?
  - **Can I get you anything to** read?
    읽으실 것 좀 가져다드릴까요?

- **I'll have …** ~ 로 주세요
  - **I'll have** a grape juice.
    포도 주스 한 잔 주세요.
  - **I'll have** the steak with mashed potatoes.
    스테이크와 으깬 감자로 주세요.

▬ STUDY TIP

미국 내 음식점들은 마케팅 차원에서 손님들이 많지 않은 시간대, 우리나라에서 주로 갖는 브레이크 타임 대신 주로 오후 3~6시에 특정 메뉴 항목을 할인하는 행사를 하는데 이를 Happy Hour(해피 아워)라고 한다.

대화를 들어보세요. 그런 다음 롤플레잉을 해보세요.

> Everything looks delicious!
> 모든 것이 맛있어 보이네요!

The ¹couple look at their menus.
부부는 메뉴를 본다.

> Can I get you anything to drink?
> 마실 것 좀 드릴까요?

apron 앞치마

The waiter asks if they would like anything to drink.
웨이터는 그들이 마실 것을 원하는지 물어본다.

> I'll have a grape juice.
> 저는 포도 주스 한 잔 주세요.

necklace 목걸이

Mary orders her drink.
Mary는 마실 것을 주문한다.

> What do you think, ⁴honey?
> 여보, 당신은 어때?

> Let's get the ⁵calamari.
> 칼라마리 먹죠.

The couple look at the menu and ⁶decides.
부부는 메뉴를 보고 결정한다.

> Hello! My name is Stuart. I'll be your waiter this evening.
> 안녕하세요! Stuart입니다. 오늘 저녁 손님들을 모실 웨이터입니다.

> Hello.
> 안녕하세요.

> Hi.
> 안녕하세요.

The waiter arrives and introduces himself.
웨이터가 와서 자신을 소개한다.

> I'd like a ²lemonade, please.
> 저는 레모네이드 주세요.

> Sure. And for you, ma'am?
> 알겠습니다. 부인께는 무엇을 드릴까요?

John orders a lemonade.
John은 레모네이드를 주문한다.

> Would you like an ³appetizer?
> 애피타이저 드시겠어요?

The waiter asks if they would like an appetizer.
웨이터는 그들이 애피타이저를 원하는지 물어본다.

> OK, I'll be right back with your drinks.
> 알겠습니다. 음료를 곧 가져오겠습니다.

The waiter leaves.
웨이터는 떠난다.

MATCHING

올바른 영영 뜻을 B열에서 찾아 A열 옆에 쓰세요.

A	B
_____ 1. appetizer	a. a drink made from lemons and sugar 레모네이드
_____ 2. calamari	b. a small amount of food served before a meal 전채
_____ 3. couple	c. to make a choice 결정하다
_____ 4. decide	d. two people who are married or dating 커플
_____ 5. lemonade	e. fried pieces of squid 칼라마리

CONVERSATION

올바른 영어 표현으로 쓰고 말해보세요.

Everything looks
1 _____!
모든 것이 맛있어 보이네요!

Hello! My name is Stuart. I'll be your waiter 2 _____.
안녕하세요! Stuart입니다. 오늘 저녁 손님들을 모실 웨이터입니다.

Hello.   Hi.

Can I get you
3 _____?
마실 것 좀 드릴까요?

4 _____
a lemonade, please.
저는 레모네이드 주세요.

Sure. And for you, ma'am?

I'll have a 5 _____.
저는 포도 주스 한 잔 주세요.

Would you like an appetizer?

What do you think, honey?

6 _____ the calamari.
칼라마리 먹죠.

OK, I'll 7 _____
with your drinks.
알겠습니다. 음료를 곧 가져오겠습니다.

RESTAURANT
DAY 23
웨이터가 돌아오다
The Waiter Returns

KEY VOCABULARY

steak	스테이크
rare	살짝 익힌
potato	감자
soup	수프
side dish	사이드 디쉬 (곁들임 요리, 반찬)
dressing	(요리용) 드레싱
seafood	해산물
spaghetti	스파게티
crab	게
squid	오징어
clam	조개
onion soup	양파 수프

KEY EXPRESSIONS

- **Are you ready …?**
  ~ 하시겠어요?
  - **Are you ready** to order?
    주문하시겠어요?
  - **Are you ready** for your next dish?
    다음 요리를 드시겠어요?

- **How would you like …?**
  ~ 을 어떻게 해드릴까요?
  - **How would you like** that?
    어떻게 해드릴까요?
  - **How would you like** your steak?
    스테이크를 어떻게 해드릴까요?

- **We have …, …, and …**
  ~ 와 ~ 와 ~ 가 있습니다.
  - **We have** French, Ranch, Thousand Island, **and** Italian dressing.
    프렌치, 랜치, 사우전 아일랜드, 그리고 이탈리안 드레싱이 있습니다.
  - **We have** black beans, refried beans, **and** pinto beans.
    검정콩, 삶아서 튀긴 콩, 강낭콩이 있습니다.

- **What's in your …?**
  ~ 에는 무엇이 들어가죠?
  - **What's in your** seafood spaghetti?
    해산물 스파게티에는 무엇이 들어가죠?
  - **What's in your** onion soup?
    양파 수프에는 무엇이 들어가죠?

STUDY TIP

스테이크 굽기 정도:

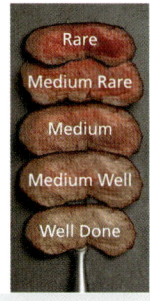

Rare / Medium Rare / Medium / Medium Well / Well Done

대화를 들어보세요. 그런 다음 롤플레잉을 해보세요.

Here you are.
여기 있습니다.

The waiter brings the drinks and the appetizer.
웨이터가 마실 것과 애피타이저를 가져온다.

Are you ready to order?
주문하시겠어요?

Yes, I'll have the New York [1]steak.
네. 저는 뉴욕 스테이크로 할래요.

The couple is ready to order.
부부는 주문할 준비가 되어있다.

How would you like that?
어떻게 해드릴까요?

Medium [2]rare, please.
미디엄 레어로 부탁해요.

The waiter asks Mary how she would like her steak cooked.
웨이터는 Mary에게 스테이크를 얼마나 익힐지 물어본다.

OK. That comes with a [3]potato, [4]soup, or salad.
네. 거기에는 감자, 수프 또는 샐러드가 곁들여 나옵니다.

I'll have a salad, please.
샐러드로 주세요.

The waiter tells Mary about the [5]side dishes.
웨이터는 Mary에게 사이드 디쉬를 소개한다.

We have French, Ranch, Thousand Island, and Italian [6]dressing.
드레싱에는 프렌치, 랜치, 사우전 아이랜드, 그리고 이탈리안 드레싱이 있습니다.

Ranch, please.
랜치로 주세요.

What's in your [7]seafood [8]spaghetti?
해산물 스파게티에는 무엇이 들어가죠?

[9]Crab, [10]squid, and [11]clams.
게, 오징어, 조개가 들어갑니다.

The waiter asks her what kind of dressing she wants.
웨이터는 그녀가 원하는 드레싱을 물어본다.

John asks about the dish he wants.
John은 자신이 원하는 요리에 대해 물어본다.

OK, I'll have that with a cup of [12]onion soup.
좋아요. 양파 수프와 함께 그것으로 하겠습니다.

John tells the waiter what side dish he wants.
John은 자신이 원하는 사이드 디쉬를 웨이터에게 말한다.

Will that be all?
그게 전부이신가요?

Yes, thanks.
네. 그렇습니다.

OK, call me if you need anything else.
알겠습니다. 더 필요하신 거 있으시면 불러주십시오.

The waiter takes the menus.
웨이터는 메뉴판을 가져간다.

MATCHING

올바른 영영 뜻을 B열에서 찾아 A열 옆에 쓰세요.

A

____ 1. crab
____ 2. dressing
____ 3. rare
____ 4. spaghetti
____ 5. steak

B

a. a sea animal with a hard shell 게
b. cooked for a minimum period of time, often referring to meat 살짝 익힌
c. long noodles, often eaten with tomato sauce 스파게티
d. sauce that is added to a salad (요리용) 드레싱
e. a thick piece of meat, usually beef 스테이크

CONVERSATION

올바른 영어 표현으로 쓰고 말해보세요.

Here you are.

Are you ready 1 _____?
주문하시겠어요?

Yes, I'll 2 _____ the New York steak.
네, 저는 뉴욕 스테이크로 할래요.

3 _____ like that?
어떻게 해드릴까요?

Medium rare, please.

OK. That 4 _____ a potato, soup, or salad.
네, 거기에는 감자, 수프 또는 샐러드가 곁들여 나옵니다.

I'll have a salad, please.

We have French, Ranch, Thousand Island, and Italian dressing.

Ranch, please.

What's in your 5 _____?
해산물 스파게티에는 무엇이 들어가죠?

Crab, squid, and clams.

OK, I'll have that with a cup of 6 _____.
좋아요. 양파 수프와 함께 그것으로 하겠습니다.

Will that be all?

Yes, thanks.

OK, 7 _____ if you need anything else.
알겠습니다. 더 필요하신 거 있으시면 불러주십시오.

RESTAURANT
DAY 24
음식이 도착하다
The Food Arrives

▬ KEY VOCABULARY

here you are	(자) 여기 (있어)
cut into	~을 칼로 자르다
parmesan cheese	파르메산 치즈
take away	치우다, 제거하다
plate	접시
dish	(식사의 일부로 만든) 요리

▬ KEY EXPRESSIONS

- **Is … all right?** ~는 괜찮으세요?
  - **Is** your steak **all right?**
    스테이크 괜찮으세요?
  - **Is** your meal **all right?**
    식사는 괜찮으세요?

- **It's … (형용사)** ~ 하네요.
  - **It's** perfect.
    좋네요.
  - **It's** great.
    훌륭하네요.

- **Would you like …?**
  ~ 해드릴까요?
  - **Would you like** some parmesan on your pasta?
    파스타에 파르메산 치즈 넣어드릴까요?
  - **Would you like** a refill?
    리필해드릴까요?

- **I'll take … away.**
  제가 ~ 을 치우겠습니다.
  - **I'll take** these plates **away.**
    이 접시들은 치우겠습니다.
  - **I'll take** your cups **away.**
    이 컵들을 치우겠습니다.

▬ STUDY TIP

다양한 음식점 종류:

bistro
작은 규모의 음식점을 의미하며, cafe보다 식당 성격이 조금 더 강한 곳

cafeteria
식당이라는 의미가 강하며 회사 구내식당이나 학교의 학생 식당을 표현할 때 주로 사용

cafe
우리나라에서는 커피숍으로 통용되지만, 미국에서는 샌드위치, 디저트, 간단한 아침을 먹을 수 있는 식당으로의 의미가 내포되어 있음

restaurant
우리말로 레스토랑은 약간 고급스러운 곳을 의미하지만, 영어로는 그냥 음식점이라는 넓은 의미로 사용

대화를 들어보세요. 그런 다음 롤플레잉을 해보세요.

The waiter brings the food.
웨이터가 음식을 가져온다.

> ¹Here you are. New York steak… and for you, sir, seafood spaghetti.
> 음식 나왔습니다. 뉴욕 스테이크… 그리고 손님은, 해산물 스파게티고요.

He puts the food on the table.
그는 음식을 테이블에 올려놓는다.

> Is your steak all right?
> 스테이크 괜찮으세요?

The waiter asks Mary about her steak.
웨이터는 Mary에게 스테이크가 어떤지 물어본다.

> Yes, it's perfect.
> 네, 아주 좋군요.

Mary ²cuts into her steak.
Mary는 스테이크를 자른다.

> Would you like some parmesan on your pasta?
> 파스타에 파르메산 치즈를 넣어드릴까요?

> Sure!
> 네.

bowl 사발

The waiter offers John some ³parmesan cheese.
웨이터는 John에게 파르메산 치즈를 권한다.

> I'll ⁴take these ⁵plates away.
> 이 접시들은 치우겠습니다.

The waiter takes the appetizer ⁶dishes from the table.
웨이터는 애피타이저 접시를 치운다.

> No, thanks.
> 아니요. 감사합니다.

> Can I get you anything else?
> 더 필요하신 것은 없으세요?

The waiter asks if they need anything else.
웨이터는 그들이 더 필요한 것은 없는지 물어본다.

> OK, then. Enjoy your meal.
> 네. 그럼 맛있게 드세요.

The waiter tells them to have a nice meal.
웨이터는 그들에게 좋은 식사 시간이 되라고 말한다.

MATCHING

올바른 영영 뜻을 B열에서 찾아 A열 옆에 쓰세요.

A	B
____ 1. cut into	a. used when giving something to someone (자) 여기 (있어)
____ 2. dish	b. to use a knife to divide something ~을 칼로 자르다
____ 3. parmesan cheese	c. a type of food 요리
____ 4. here you are	d. to move something to another place 치우다
____ 5. take away	e. a hard and dry cheese 파르메산 치즈

CONVERSATION

올바른 영어 표현으로 쓰고 말해보세요.

Here you are. New York steak... and for you, sir, 1 _____.
음식 나왔습니다. 뉴욕 스테이크... 그리고 손님은, 해산물 스파게티고요.

Is your steak 2 _____?
스테이크 괜찮으세요?

Yes, it's perfect.

Would you like some parmesan 3 _____?
파스타에 파르메산 치즈를 넣어드릴까요?

Sure!

I'll take 4 _____ away.
이 접시들은 치우겠습니다.

No, thanks.

Can I get you 5 _____?
더 필요하신 것은 없으세요?

OK, then. 6 _____ your meal.
네. 그럼 맛있게 드세요.

RESTAURANT
DAY 25
맛있는 식사
A Lovely Meal

KEY VOCABULARY

dessert (syn. afters, sweet)	디저트, 후식
full	배부르게 먹은
decline	거절하다, 사양하다
rest	나머지
take-home box	포장 박스
wrap up	싸다, 포장하다

KEY EXPRESSIONS

- **Could we have ..., please?**
  ~를 주시겠어요?
  - **Could we have** the bill**, please?**
    계산서 주시겠어요?
  - **Could we have** the check**, please?**
    계산서 주시겠어요?

- **Here's your ...** 여기 ~ 있습니다.
  - **Here's your** bill.
    여기 계산서가 있습니다.
  - **Here's your** water.
    여기 물이 있습니다.

- **Could I take ...?** ~을 가져가도 될까요?
  - **Could I take** the rest home**?**
    나머지는 집으로 가져가도 될까요?
  - **Could I take** all of this home**?**
    이거 다 집으로 가져가도 될까요?

- **... be satisfied with ...**
  ~는 ~에 만족하다.
  - John and Mary **are** very **satisfied with** the meal.
    John과 Mary는 식사에 매우 만족했다.
  - We **are** all **satisfied with** our food.
    우리는 모두 음식에 만족한다.

STUDY TIP

미국의 거의 모든 식당에는 남은 음식을 싸 갈 수 있는 박스가 준비되어 있다. 접시를 비우면 점원이 와서 접시를 가져가거나, 계속 음식을 남겨두고 얘기를 한다면 점원이 직접 다가와 포장 박스가 필요한지 묻곤 한다.

대화를 들어보세요. 그런 다음 롤플레잉을 해보세요.

The waiter asks about dessert.
웨이터는 후식에 대해 물어본다.

Mary ³declines.
Mary가 사양한다.

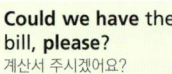

John asks for the bill.
John은 계산서를 요청한다.

The waiter brings the bill.
웨이터는 계산서를 가지고 온다.

Mary asks for a ⁵take-home box.
Mary는 포장 박스를 요청한다.

The waiter takes the plates from the table.
웨이터는 테이블에서 음식이 들어 있는 접시를 가져간다.

John and Mary **are** very **satisfied with** the meal.
John과 Mary는 식사에 매우 만족했다.

The waiter comes back with the take-home box.
웨이터는 포장 박스를 가지고 돌아온다.

MATCHING

올바른 영영 뜻을 B열에서 찾아 A열 옆에 쓰세요.

A	B
___ 1. decline	a. not hungry anymore 배부르게 먹은
___ 2. dessert	b. to say no to something 거절하다
___ 3. full	c. a box that holds leftover food 포장 박스
___ 4. rest	d. a sweet food that is eaten after a meal 후식
___ 5. take-home box	e. things that were not used or not eaten 나머지

CONVERSATION

올바른 영어 표현으로 쓰고 말해보세요.

1 _____ dessert this evening?
후식 주문하시겠어요?

No, thanks. We're 2 _____ !
고맙지만, 됐습니다. 배가 불러요!

3 _____ the bill, please?
계산서 주시겠어요?

Here's your bill.

I couldn't eat everything. Could I 4 _____ home?
다 못 먹었어요. 나머지는 집으로 가져갈 수 있을까요?

Sure. I'll wrap it up for you. Let me 5 _____ .
물론입니다. 제가 싸드릴게요. 손님 접시를 가져가겠습니다.

That was an 6 _____ .
정말 훌륭한 저녁 식사였어.

Yes, it was.

Here you are.

SECTION 5 RESTAURANT

SECTION 6

Airport

비행기 타고 내리기

| DAY 26 | Check-in
탑승 수속

| DAY 27 | Security
보안 검색

| DAY 28 | Boarding
탑승

| DAY 29 | The Flight
비행

| DAY 30 | Immigration (Arrival)
입국심사 (도착)

AIRPORT
DAY 26
탑승 수속
Check-in

▬ KEY VOCABULARY

passport	여권
mileage card	마일리지 카드
luggage	(여행용) 짐, 수화물
scale	저울
pack	(짐을) 싸다, 꾸리다
suitcase	여행 가방
unattended	주인이 옆에 있지 않은, 방치된
airline agent	항공사 직원
attach (ant. detach)	붙이다
ID tag	ID 태그
aisle seat	통로 자리
window seat	창가 자리
boarding pass	탑승권
receive	받다, 받아들이다

▬ KEY EXPRESSIONS

- **Can I see ..., please?** ~를 보여주실래요?
  - **Can I see** your passport and ticket, **please?**
    여권과 비행기표를 보여주실래요?
  - **Can I see** your plane ticket, **please?**
    비행기표 보여주실래요?
- **Did you pack ...?** ~을 싸셨나요?
  - **Did you pack** your own suitcase?
    여행 가방 직접 싸셨나요?
  - **Did you pack** your bags yourself?
    가방 직접 싸셨나요?
- **I'd like ..., please.** ~로 부탁합니다.
  - **I'd like** a window seat, **please.**
    창 쪽으로 부탁합니다.
  - **I'd like** a seat in the back, **please.**
    뒤쪽으로 부탁합니다.

▬ STUDY TIP

기내 수하물과 위탁 수하물:

기내 수하물은 말 그대로 비행기 안에 직접 가지고 타는 수하물이고 위탁 수하물은 비행기 짐칸으로 보내는 수하물을 말한다. 위탁 수하물의 경우 공항에 도착한 후 체크인 시 미리 맡기게 된다.

대화를 들어보세요. 그런 다음 롤플레잉을 해보세요.

Kim goes to the check-in counter.
Kim은 수속 카운터로 간다.

Kim shows her mileage club card.
Kim은 마일리지 클럽 카드를 제시한다.

Kim puts her luggage on the ⁴scale.
Kim은 수하물을 저울에 올려놓는다.

The ⁸airline agent asks Kim about her luggage.
항공사 직원은 Kim에게 여행 가방에 대해 물어본다.

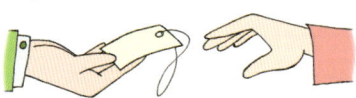

Kim gets a luggage ¹⁰ID tag.
Kim은 수하물 확인 꼬리표를 받는다.

Kim chooses a seat.
Kim은 좌석을 선택한다.

Kim ¹⁴receives her boarding pass.
Kim은 탑승권을 받는다.

The airline agent points Kim in the right direction.
항공사 직원은 Kim에게 방향을 알려 준다.

MATCHING

올바른 영영 뜻을 B열에서 찾아 A열 옆에 쓰세요.

A	B
____ 1. aisle seat	a. a chair next to a window 창가 자리
____ 2. boarding pass	b. a chair next to a walkway 통로 자리
____ 3. luggage	c. the bags you bring when you travel 수하물
____ 4. receive	d. to get 받다
____ 5. window seat	e. a ticket you need to get onto an airplane 탑승권

CONVERSATION

올바른 영어 표현으로 쓰고 말해보세요.

Good morning. Can I see your 1 _____, please?
안녕하세요. 여권과 비행기표를 보여주실래요?

Here you are.

Here is my 2 _____.
제 마일리지 카드 여기 있습니다.

Do you have any 3 _____ to check?
수하물 있으신가요?

Yes, this suitcase.

Please put it 4 _____.
저울에 올려 주세요.

5 _____ your own suitcase?
여행 가방을 직접 싸셨나요?

Yes, I did.

Have you 6 _____ unattended since you packed it?
가방을 싸신 후 방치한 적 있나요?

No, I haven't.

Please 7 _____ on this and attach it to your suitcase.
여기에 이름을 쓰셔서 가방에 붙여주세요.

Would you like a window or an aisle seat?

I'd like 8 _____, please.
창 쪽으로 부탁합니다.

Here is your boarding pass. Your 9 _____ is 10 o'clock.
탑승권을 받으세요.
탑승 시각은 10시입니다.

Gate 15 is down the hall to the left.

Thank you. Good-bye.

DAY 27

AIRPORT

보안 검색
Security

KEY VOCABULARY

film	필름
empty	비우다
pocket	주머니
step	(발걸음을 떼어놓아) 움직이다
security guard	보안 요원
aspirin	아스피린
headache	두통
pill	알약, 정제
immigration	공항 출입국 심사대, 출입국 관리소
head for	~으로 향하다
stamp	(도장 스탬프 등을) 찍다

KEY EXPRESSIONS

- **Please empty ...** ~을 모두 꺼내주세요.
  - **Please empty** your pockets.
    주머니에 있는 것을 모두 꺼내주세요.
  - **Please empty** your bag.
    가방에 있는 것을 모두 꺼내주세요.

- **Can I look through ...?**
  ~을 살펴봐도 될까요?
  - **Can I look through** your bag?
    가방을 살펴봐도 될까요?
  - **Can I look through** your laptop?
    노트북을 살펴봐도 될까요?

- **They're ... for ...** ~에 ~할 ~입니다.
  - **They're** aspirin **for** headaches.
    두통에 먹을 아스피린입니다.
  - **They're** pills **for** thyroid.
    갑상선 약들입니다.

- **Please go to ...** ~로 가세요.
  - **Please go to** immigration now.
    이제 출국심사대로 가세요.
  - **Please go to** customs.
    세관으로 가세요.

STUDY TIP

보안 검사에서 쓰일 수 있는 다양한 표현들:

Please go through the detector.
탐지기를 통과해주세요.

Please take off your shoes and belt.
신발과 허리띠 다 벗어주세요.

Do I have to take out all my belongings?
소지품 다 꺼내야 하나요?

I don't have anything in my pocket.
주머니에 아무것도 없습니다.

대화를 들어보세요. 그런 다음 롤플레잉을 해보세요.

Kim puts her bag through the X-ray machine.
Kim은 자신의 가방을 엑스레이 투시기에 통과시킨다.

Kim puts her keys in the tray.
Kim은 열쇠를 바구니에 놓는다.

Kim walks through the metal detector.
Kim은 금속 탐지기를 통과한다.

The ⁵security guard picks up Kim's bag.
보안요원이 Kim의 가방을 손에 든다.

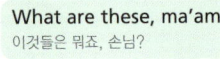

The security guard looks at Kim's ⁸pills.
보안요원은 Kim의 알약을 살펴본다.

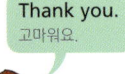

Kim ¹⁰heads for immigration.
Kim은 출국심사대로 간다.

Kim gives her passport to the immigration officer.
Kim은 출국심사대 직원에게 여권을 건넨다.

The immigration officer ¹¹stamps Kim's passport.
출국심사대 직원은 Kim의 여권에 도장을 찍는다.

MATCHING

올바른 영영 뜻을 B열에서 찾아 A열 옆에 쓰세요.

A
1. aspirin
2. empty
3. head for
4. headache
5. stamp

B
a. to remove all things from something 비우다
b. pain in your head 두통
c. a medicine you can take for pain or fever 아스피린
d. to go toward ~으로 향하다
e. to mark something using a tool and ink (도장 스탬프 등을) 찍다

CONVERSATION

올바른 영어 표현으로 쓰고 말해보세요.

AIRPORT
DAY 28
탑승
Boarding

KEY VOCABULARY

proceed	(특정 방향으로) 이동하다
gate	탑승구
row	열, 줄
flight attendant	승무원
get by (syn. pass)	지나가다
stand up	일어나다
let by	~을 통과시키다
make sure	확실하게 하다
fasten	매다, 잠그다

KEY EXPRESSIONS

- **We will now begin boarding …**
  ~ 탑승을 시작하겠습니다.
  - **We will now begin boarding** rows 20-40.
    20에서 40번 좌석 탑승을 시작하겠습니다.
  - **We will now begin boarding** all first-class passengers.
    일등석 승객부터 좌석 탑승을 시작하겠습니다.

- **Would you like me to …?**
  ~ 해드릴까요?
  - **Would you like me** to put up your bag?
    가방 올려드릴까요?
  - **Would you like me** to get you some water?
    물을 좀 가져다드릴까요?

- **I'd like to …** ~ 할게요.
  - **I'd like to** keep it with me.
    제가 가지고 있을게요.
  - **I'd like to** put it in storage.
    창고에 넣을게요.

- **Please make sure …** ~ 해 주세요.
  - **Please make sure** your seat belt is fastened.
    안전벨트 매주세요.
  - **Please make sure** all seats are upright.
    모든 좌석을 똑바로 세워주세요.

STUDY TIP

공항과 기내에서 들을 수 있는 다양한 단어들:

stopover (여정 상의 두 지점 사이에 잠시) 머묾, 단기 체류
중간 기착지에서 환승하는 시간이 길어 그곳에서 8시간 혹은 하루 이상을 넘기는 경우, 이 경우에는 입국했다가 다시 출국하는 절차를 거쳐야 함

transit 환승
급유, 정비 등을 위해 승객이 비행기에서 내려 공항 빌딩으로 나가 1시간 이상 대합실에서 기다리는 경우로 동일한 비행기를 다시 타고 감

transfer 환승
중간 기착지에 내려 다른 비행기로 갈아타는 것

대화를 들어보세요. 그런 다음 롤플레잉을 해보세요.

> Ladies and gentlemen, World Air Flight 225 to London is now ready for boarding. Please ¹proceed to Gate 15 at this time.
> 여러분, 런던행 월드에어 225편 항공기는 탑승 준비가 되었습니다. 15번 탑승구로 가십시오.

Kim hurries to the ²gate.
Kim은 탑승구로 서둘러 간다.

> We will now begin boarding ³rows 20-40.
> 20에서 40번 좌석 탑승을 시작하겠습니다.

Kim checks her boarding pass.
Kim은 탑승권을 확인한다.

> Boarding pass please.
> 탑승권 주세요.
>
> Here you are.
> 여기 있습니다.
>
> Thank you.
> 고맙습니다.

Kim gives her boarding pass to the airline agent.
Kim은 탑승권을 항공사 직원에게 준다.

> Where is seat 36J?
> 좌석번호 36J는 어디죠?
>
> Just go straight and it's on the right.
> 곧바로 가서, 오른쪽에 있습니다.

Kim gets on the plane.
Kim은 비행기에 탑승한다.

> Would you like me to put up your bag?
> 가방 올려 드릴까요?
>
> No, thank you. I'd like to keep it with me.
> 아니요, 고맙습니다. 가지고 있을게요.

overhead compartment 좌석 위의 수납공간

The ⁴flight attendant offers to help Kim.
승무원이 Kim에게 도와주겠다고 한다.

> Excuse me, sir. Could I ⁵get by? That's my seat by the window.
> 실례합니다, 선생님. 지나갈 수 있을까요? 창 쪽이 제 좌석이거든요.

Kim moves to her seat.
Kim은 자신의 좌석으로 이동한다.

> Thanks a lot.
> 고맙습니다.
>
> No problem.
> 괜찮습니다.

The man ⁶stands up to ⁷let Kim by.
남자는 Kim이 지나갈 수 있도록 일어선다.

> Please ⁸make sure your seat belt is ⁹fastened, ma'am.
> 안전벨트 매주세요, 손님.
>
> OK.
> 네.

buckle 버클
seat belt 안전벨트

Kim buckles her seat belt.
Kim은 안전벨트를 맨다.

MATCHING

올바른 영영 뜻을 B열에서 찾아 A열 옆에 쓰세요.

A	B
_____ 1. flight attendant	a. to check something 확실하게 하다
_____ 2. gate	b. to rise from your chair 일어나다
_____ 3. make sure	c. a place in an airport where people get on or off an airplane 탑승구
_____ 4. proceed	d. a person who serves people on an airplane 승무원
_____ 5. stand up	e. to move forward toward something (특정 방향으로) 이동하다

CONVERSATION

올바른 영어 표현으로 쓰고 말해보세요.

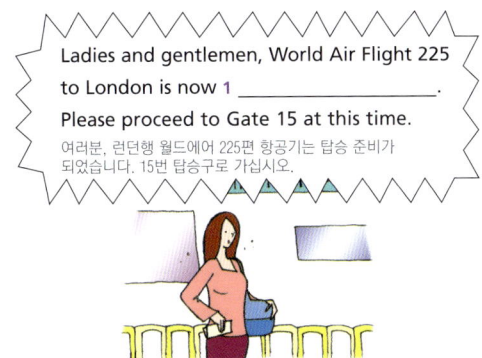

Ladies and gentlemen, World Air Flight 225 to London is now 1 _____.
Please proceed to Gate 15 at this time.
여러분, 런던행 월드에어 225편 항공기는 탑승 준비가 되었습니다. 15번 탑승구로 가십시오.

We will now begin boarding 2 _____.
20에서 40번 좌석 탑승을 시작하겠습니다.

Boarding pass please.
Here you are.
Thank you.

Where is 3 _____?
좌석번호 36J는 어디죠?

Just 4 _____ and it's on the right.
곧바로 가서, 오른쪽에 있습니다.

Would you like me to 5 _____?
가방 올려 드릴까요?

No, thank you. I'd like to keep it with me.

Excuse me, sir. Could I 6 _____?
That's my seat by the window.
실례합니다, 선생님. 지나갈 수 있을까요? 창 쪽이 제 좌석이거든요.

Thanks a lot.
No problem.

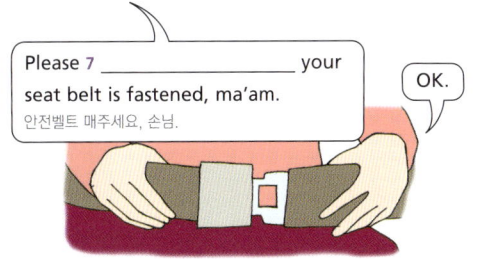

Please 7 _____ your seat belt is fastened, ma'am.
안전벨트 매주세요, 손님.
OK.

AIRPORT
DAY 29
비행
The Flight

▬ KEY VOCABULARY

on business	업무로
on vacation	휴가로
discuss (syn. talk, speak)	말을 주고받다
parents	부모
serve	(식당 등에서 음식을) 제공하다
chicken	닭고기
captain	(항공기의) 기장
experience	겪다
turbulence	난기류, 난류
hear	듣다, 들리다
announcement	안내 방송, 발표
landing (ant. takeoff)	착륙
get off	(타고 있던 것에서) 내리다

▬ KEY EXPRESSIONS

- **Is this your first time …?**
  ~ 가 처음인가요?
  - **Is this your first time** to England?
    영국은 처음인가요?
  - **Is this your first time** to Toronto?
    토론토는 처음인가요?

- **I'm going to …**   ~ 할 예정이에요.
  - **I'm going to** visit my parents in Manchester.
    맨체스터에 계신 부모님을 방문할 예정이에요.
  - **I'm going to** see some family.
    가족들을 만날 예정이에요.

- **Would you like … or …?**
  ~ 와 ~ 중 어느 것으로 하시겠어요?
  - **Would you like** chicken **or** seafood?
    닭고기와 해산물 중 어느 것을 드시겠어요?
  - **Would you like** the Western meal **or** the Korean meal?
    양식과 한식 중 어느 것으로 하시겠어요?

▬ STUDY TIP

'get off'의 다양한 쓰임:

1. 떠나다
We got off right after breakfast.
우리는 아침밥을 먹고 바로 떠났다.

2. (타고 있는 것에서) 내리다
When you get off the bus, please check your belongings.
버스에서 내릴 때는 소지품을 확인하세요.

3. (직장에서) 퇴근하다
I can't get off early today. I have so much work to do.
나 오늘 일찍 퇴근 못 해. 할 일이 너무 많아.

대화를 들어보세요. 그런 다음 롤플레잉을 해보세요.

Is this your first time to England?
영국은 처음인가요?

Yes.
네.

Are you traveling ¹on business?
업무차 가시는 건가요?

No, I'm just going ²on vacation. How about you?
아니요. 그냥 휴가로 가는 거예요. 당신은요?

Kim chats with the passenger next to her.
Kim은 옆 좌석의 승객과 가벼운 얘기를 나눈다.

They ³discuss their travel plans.
그들은 여행 계획에 대해 얘기를 나눈다.

I'm going to visit my ⁴parents in Manchester.
저는 맨체스터에 계신 부모님을 방문할 예정이에요.

arm rest
팔걸이

The man puts his seat back.
남자는 좌석을 뒤로 젖힌다.

What would you like to drink?
음료는 뭐로 드시겠어요?

I'll have some orange juice, please.
오렌지주스 부탁합니다.

The flight attendants ⁵serve drinks.
승무원들이 마실 것을 제공한다.

This is your ⁷captain speaking. We are ⁸experiencing some ⁹turbulence. Please return to your seats and fasten your seat belts.
기장입니다. 난기류를 통과하는 중입니다. 좌석으로 가셔서 안전벨트를 매주시기 바랍니다.

Excuse me ma'am. Would you like ⁶chicken or seafood?
실례합니다, 손님. 닭고기와 해산물 중 어느 것을 드시겠어요?

I will have chicken, please.
닭고기로 부탁합니다.

tray table
식사 테이블

Kim pulls down her tray table.
Kim은 식사 테이블을 당겨 편다.

Kim ¹⁰hears the captain's ¹¹announcement.
Kim은 기장의 안내 방송을 듣는다.

Sir, please put your seat up for ¹²landing.
손님, 착륙하려고 하니 등받이를 세워주시기 바랍니다.

Sorry.
미안합니다.

Thank you for flying World Air. Have a nice day.
월드에어 항공을 이용해주셔서 감사합니다. 좋은 하루 되시기 바랍니다.

Bye-bye.
안녕히 계세요.

The man puts his seat back up.
남자는 좌석 등받이를 세운다.

Kim ¹³gets off the plane.
Kim은 비행기에서 내린다.

MATCHING

올바른 영영 뜻을 B열에서 찾아 A열 옆에 쓰세요.

A

_____ 1. captain
_____ 2. discuss
_____ 3. parents
_____ 4. serve
_____ 5. turbulence

B

a. a person who is in charge of an airplane (항공기의) 기장
b. to talk about something 말을 주고받다
c. strong winds that happen suddenly 난기류
d. your mother and father 부모
e. to give someone food or a drink (식당 등에서 음식을) 제공하다

CONVERSATION

올바른 영어 표현으로 쓰고 말해보세요.

AIRPORT
DAY 30

입국심사 (도착)
Immigration (Arrival)

■ KEY VOCABULARY

arrival card	입국신고서
scan	(스캐너로) 스캔하다
stay	머물다, 지내다, 묵다
purpose	목적, 의도
continue	계속되다, 계속하다
baggage claim	수하물 찾는 곳
pleasant	즐거운, 쾌적한

■ KEY EXPRESSIONS

- **I flew in from ...** ~에서 왔습니다.
  - **I flew in from** New York.
    뉴욕에서 왔습니다.
  - **I flew in from** St. Petersburg.
    상트페테르부르크에서 왔습니다.
- **How long will you be ...?** 얼마 동안 ~ 하실 거죠?
  - **How long will you be** staying in London?
    런던에 얼마 동안 머무르실 거죠?
  - **How long will you be** in the country?
    시골에 얼마나 계실 거죠?
- **I'll be here for ...** ~ 동안 머무를 겁니다.
  - **I'll be here for** 10 days.
    열흘 동안 머무를 겁니다.
  - **I'll be here for** a week.
    일주일 동안 머무를 겁니다.
- **I'm just here ...** 여기 ~ 하러 왔어요.
  - **I'm just here** on vacation.
    휴가차 왔어요.
  - **I'm just here** on business.
    사업차 왔어요.

■ STUDY TIP

입국 심사할 때 자주 사용되는 표현:

May I see your passport, please?
여권 보여주세요.

What is your final destination?
최종 목적지가 어디인가요?

How long are you going to stay?
얼마나 머무실 건가요?

Where are you going to stay?
어디서 머무실 건가요?

대화를 들어보세요. 그런 다음 롤플레잉을 해보세요.

Next, please!
다음 분 오세요!

Kim steps up to the immigration desk.
Kim은 입국심사대로 다가선다.

Good afternoon, miss. Passport and ¹arrival card, please.
여권과 입국신고서 주세요.

Here you are.
여기 있습니다.

Kim hands her passport and card to the officer.
Kim은 여권과 입국신고서를 직원에게 건넨다.

Where are you coming from?
어디에서 오셨나요?

I flew in from New York.
뉴욕에서 왔습니다.

scanner
스캐너

The officer ²scans the arrival card.
직원은 입국신고서를 스캔한다.

How long will you be ³staying in London?
런던에 얼마 동안 머무르실 거죠?

I'll be here for 10 days.
열흘 동안 머무를 겁니다.

He looks at Kim's passport.
그는 Kim의 여권을 살펴본다.

What is the ⁴purpose of your visit?
방문 목적은 무엇이죠?

I'm just here on vacation.
휴가차 왔어요.

The officer ⁵continues to ask her questions.
직원은 그녀에게 계속 질문한다.

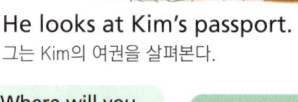

Where will you be staying?
어디에 머무르실 거죠?

I'll be staying at the Plaza Hotel.
플라자 호텔입니다.

The officer enters some information into the computer.
직원은 정보를 컴퓨터에 입력한다.

All right. You may proceed to the ⁶baggage claim.
좋습니다. 수하물 찾는 곳으로 가셔도 됩니다.

Have a ⁷pleasant stay in London.
런던에서 즐겁게 보내세요.

Thank you very much.
고맙습니다.

stamp
도장

The officer stamps Kim's passport.
직원은 Kim의 여권에 도장을 찍는다.

Kim takes back her passport.
Kim은 여권을 돌려받는다.

MATCHING

올바른 영영 뜻을 B열에서 찾아 A열 옆에 쓰세요.

A	B
_____ 1. baggage claim	a. to keep doing something 계속하다
_____ 2. continue	b. to use a machine to get information from something (스캐너로) 스캔하다
_____ 3. pleasant	c. a place in an airport where you get your bags 수하물 찾는 곳
_____ 4. purpose	d. your reason for doing something 목적
_____ 5. scan	e. very nice; very good 즐거운

CONVERSATION

올바른 영어 표현으로 쓰고 말해보세요.

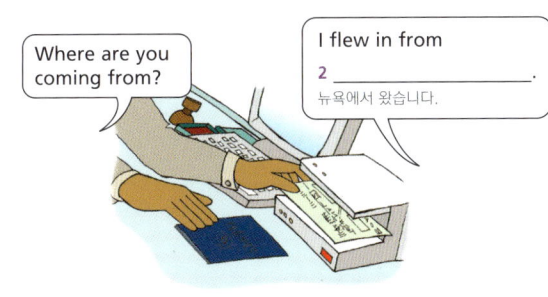

SECTION 7

Travel

관광하며 돌아다니기

DAY 31 Car Rental
차 빌리기

DAY 32 Hotel Check-in
호텔 체크인

DAY 33 The Hotel Concierge
호델 긴시이지

DAY 34 Sightseeing
관광

DAY 35 Hotel Check-out
호텔 체크아웃

TRAVEL
DAY 31
차 빌리기
Car Rental

KEY VOCABULARY

rent a car	차를 빌리다
compact car	소형 자동차
sedan	세단형 자동차
SUV	스포츠 실용차
available	이용할 수 있는, 구할 수 있는
vehicle	차량, 탈 것
form	양식, 서식
international	국제적인
driver's license	운전면허증
complete	기입하다, 작성하다
insurance	보험
free map	무료 지도
accept (ant. reject)	받아들이다

KEY EXPRESSIONS

- **I'd like ...** ~로 할게요.
  - **I'd like** a compact car, please.
    소형차로 할게요.
  - **I'd like** a sedan, please.
    세단으로 할게요.

- **I'll need it for ...** ~ 동안 사용할게요.
  - **I'll need it for** 10 days.
    열흘 동안 사용할게요.
  - **I'll need it for** two weeks.
    2주 동안 사용할게요.

- **Please show us ...** ~을 보여주세요.
  - **Please show us** your international driver's license.
    국제면허증을 보여주세요.
  - **Please show us** your plane ticket.
    비행기표를 보여주세요.

STUDY TIP

영국은 파운드(Pound Sterling)라는 화폐 단위를 사용하고 보통 £ 기호로 나타낸다.

대화를 들어보세요. 그런 다음 롤플레잉을 해보세요.

Hello. How may I help you?
안녕하세요. 무엇을 도와드릴까요?

I'd like to ¹rent a car please.
차를 빌리고 싶은데요.

Ok. We have ²compact cars, ³sedans, and ⁴SUVs.
네. 저희는 소형 및 중형 승용차, 그리고 SUV 차량이 있습니다.

Kim stands at the car rental desk.
Kim은 차량 임대 데스크에 다가선다.

The agent shows Kim the ⁵available ⁶vehicles.
직원이 Kim에게 임대할 수 있는 차량을 알려준다.

I'd like a compact car, please.
소형차로 할게요.

We have a two-door car for £40 a day.
문이 두 개 달린 차는 하루에 40파운드입니다.

Sounds great. I'll need it for 10 days.
좋아요. 열흘 동안 사용할게요.

Kim chooses a car.
Kim은 차를 고른다.

Kim says how long she will need the car.
Kim은 얼마나 차를 사용할 것인지 말한다.

OK. Just fill out this ⁷form. Also, **please show us** your ⁸international ⁹driver's license.
알겠습니다. 이 신청서를 작성해 주세요. 그리고 국제면허증도 제시해 주시고요.

You can buy ¹¹insurance as well. It's £10 a day.
보험도 들 수 있어요. 하루에 10파운드에요.

That's a good idea. I'll take it.
좋아요. 들죠.

The agent gives Kim a form to ¹⁰complete.
직원은 Kim에게 작성해야 할 신청서를 준다.

The car rental agent suggests insurance.
차량 임대 직원이 보험을 권한다.

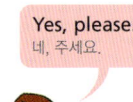
Would you like a ¹²free map?
무료 지도 필요하세요?

Yes, please.
네, 주세요.

Have a nice trip.
좋은 여행 되세요.

Thank you.
고마워요.

Kim ¹³accepts a free map from the rental agent.
Kim은 직원에게서 무료 지도를 받는다.

The car rental agent hands her the keys.
직원은 그녀에게 열쇠를 건넨다.

MATCHING

올바른 영영 뜻을 B열에서 찾아 A열 옆에 쓰세요.

A
1. accept
2. complete
3. driver's license
4. rent a car
5. SUV

B
a. a large type of car with off-road design features 스포츠 실용차
b. to say yes to something 받아들이다
c. to add information to a document 기입하다
d. to pay to borrow a car 차를 빌리다
e. a card you receive after passing a driving test 운전면허증

CONVERSATION

올바른 영어 표현으로 쓰고 말해보세요.

Hello. How may I help you?

I'd like to 1 _____, please.
차를 빌리고 싶은데요.

Ok. We have compact cars, 2 _____.
네, 저희는 소형 및 중형 승용차, 그리고 SUV 차량이 있습니다.

I'd like a 3 _____, please.
소형차로 할게요.

We have a two-door car for £40 a day.

4 _____.
I'll need it for 10 days.
좋아요. 열흘 동안 사용할게요.

OK. Just 5 _____ this form. Also, please show us your international driver's license.
알았습니다. 이 신청서를 작성해 주세요. 그리고 국제면허증도 제시해 주시고요.

You can buy 6 _____ as well. It's £10 a day.
보험도 들 수 있어요. 하루에 10파운드에요.

That's a good idea. I'll take it.

Would you like a 7 _____?
무료 지도 필요하세요?

Yes, please.

Have a 8 _____.
좋은 여행 되세요.

Thank you.

TRAVEL
DAY 32
호텔 체크인
Hotel Check-in

KEY VOCABULARY

receptionist	(호텔, 병원 등의) 접수 담당자
check in	체크인하다
single room	1인용 침실
correct (syn. right)	맞는, 정확한
information	정보
non-smoking (ant. smoking)	금연의

KEY EXPRESSIONS

- **You have (방 타입) ... for (기간) ...**
  ~을 ~ 동안 예약하셨네요.
  - **You have** a single room **for** 10 nights.
    1인실을 열흘간 예약하셨네요.
  - **You have** a double room **for** 2 days.
    2인실을 이틀간 예약하셨네요.

- **I'll use ...** ~을 사용할게요.
  - **I'll use** my credit card.
    신용카드를 사용할게요.
  - **I'll use** a check.
    수표를 사용할게요.

- **Is my room ...?** 제 방이 ~ 인가요?
  - **Is my room** a non-smoking room?
    제 방은 금연실인가요?
  - **Is my room** on the ground floor?
    제 방은 1층인가요?

STUDY TIP

호텔에 체크인할 때 사용할 수 있는 다양한 표현들:

I made a reservation under (the name of) Scarlet.
Scarlet으로 예약했어요.
바우처나 여권을 제시하면서 누구 이름으로 예약했는지 말할 때 쓸 수 있다.

Can I check in early?
체크인을 일찍 할 수 있을까요?
생각보다 호텔에 일찍 도착해서 체크인 시간이 남았을 때 물어볼 수 있는 표현이다.

Can I keep my luggage here?
여기에 제 짐을 맡겨도 될까요?
만약 일찍 도착했는데, 얼리 체크인이 안 된다면 호텔에 짐을 맡길 수 있는지 물어 볼 수 있다.

대화를 들어보세요. 그런 다음 롤플레잉을 해보세요.

Welcome to the Plaza Hotel.
어서 오세요, 플라자 호텔입니다.

Thank you.
고맙습니다.

doorman
(호텔) 현관 안내인

Kim enters the hotel.
Kim은 호텔에 들어선다.

Good afternoon. How may I help you?
안녕하세요. 무엇을 도와드릴까요?

The ¹receptionist greets Kim at the front desk.
접수 담당자가 프런트 데스크에서 Kim을 맞이한다.

Hi! I'd like to ²check in please.
안녕하세요! 체크인하고 싶은데요.

Kim puts her purse on the counter.
Kim은 지갑을 카운터에 올려놓는다.

Do you have a reservation?
예약하셨나요?

Yes. My name is Kimberly Jones.
네. 제 이름은 Kimberly Jones입니다.

Kim tells the receptionist her name.
Kim은 접수 담당자에게 이름을 말한다.

Yes.
네.

You have a ³single room for 10 nights, is that ⁴correct?
손님께서는 1인실을 열흘간 예약하셨네요. 맞습니까?

The receptionist checks the ⁵information on the computer.
접수 담당자는 예약정보를 컴퓨터에서 확인한다.

How will you pay for your room?
결제는 어떻게 하실 건가요?

I'll use my credit card.
신용카드로 하겠습니다.

Kim hands over her credit card.
Kim은 신용카드를 건넨다.

Is my room a ⁶non-smoking room?
제 방은 금연실인가요?

Yes, ma'am.
네, 그렇습니다.

That's great. Thank you.
좋아요. 고맙습니다.

Kim asks about her room.
Kim은 그녀의 방에 대해 묻는다.

You're in room 617. Enjoy your stay!
617호입니다. 편히 쉬세요!

Thank you.
고맙습니다.

Kim gets her room key.
Kim은 객실 키를 받는다.

MATCHING

올바른 영영 뜻을 B열에서 찾아 A열 옆에 쓰세요.

A	B
_____ 1. correct	a. not allowing people to smoke 금연의
_____ 2. information	b. a hotel worker who welcomes visitors and answers the phone (호텔, 병원 등의) 접수 담당자
_____ 3. non-smoking	c. a room for one person 1인용 침실
_____ 4. receptionist	d. facts about a person, place, event, etc. 정보
_____ 5. single room	e. true; not wrong 정확한

CONVERSATION

올바른 영어 표현으로 쓰고 말해보세요.

1 _____ the Plaza Hotel.
어서 오세요, 플라자 호텔입니다.

Thank you.

Good afternoon.
2 _____ help you?
안녕하세요. 무엇을 도와드릴까요?

Hi! I'd like to
3 _____ please.
안녕하세요! 체크인하고 싶은데요.

Do you have a
4 _____?
예약하셨나요?

Yes. My name is Kimberly Jones.

You have a
5 _____
for 10 nights, is that correct?
손님께서는 1인실을 열흘간 예약하셨네요. 맞습니까?

Yes.

How will you
6 _____ your room?
결제는 어떻게 하실 건가요?

I'll use my
7 _____.
신용카드로 하겠습니다.

Is my room a 8 _____?
제 방은 금연실인가요?

Yes, ma'am.

That's great. Thank you.

You're in room 617. Enjoy your stay!

Thank you.

TRAVEL
DAY 33

호텔 컨시어지
The Hotel Concierge

KEY VOCABULARY

brochure	(안내용) 책자
concierge	(호텔의) 안내원, 안내인
accent	말씨, 억양
sightseeing	관광
give a ride	태워주다
wonder	궁금하다, 궁금해하다

KEY EXPRESSIONS

- **I would like to …** ~하고 싶어요.
  - **I would like to** visit Stonehenge today.
    오늘 스톤헨지에 가고 싶은데요.
  - **I would like to** try some local food.
    현지 음식을 좀 먹어보고 싶어요.

- **Are you from …?** ~에서 오셨나요?
  - **Are you from** the States?
    미국에서 오셨나요?
  - **Are you from** Germany?
    독일에서 오셨나요?

- **Are you going … ing?** ~하실 건가요?
  - **Are you going** sightsee**ing** today?
    오늘 관광하실 건가요?
  - **Are you going** canoe**ing** today?
    오늘 카누 하러 가실 건가요?

- **Why don't we …?** ~하시겠어요?
  - **Why don't we** go together?
    같이 가시겠어요?
  - **Why don't we** stop by the hotel first?
    호텔에 먼저 들르시겠어요?

STUDY TIP

영국 런던에서 남서쪽으로 130km 떨어진 월트셔주 솔즈베리 평원에 있는 스톤헨지, 거대한 돌기둥이라고도 한다.
여러 개의 돌 중 가장 큰 것은 7m, 무게는 45톤이다.

대화를 들어보세요. 그런 다음 롤플레잉을 해보세요.

Excuse me. I would like to visit Stonehenge today.
실례합니다. 오늘 스톤헨지에 가고 싶은데요.

All right. Here is a good ¹brochure and map.
네. 여기 좋은 팸플릿과 지도가 있어요.

Kim gets some information from the ²**concierge.**
Kim은 호텔 안내원에게서 정보를 얻는다.

Pardon me. **Are you from** the States?
실례하지만, 미국에서 오셨나요?

Yes, I'm from Austin.
네, 저는 오스틴에서 왔어요.

A woman notices Kim's American ³**accent.**
한 여자가 Kim의 미국 억양을 알아차린다.

I'm Ruth, from Atlanta.
저는 Ruth에요. 애틀랜타에서 왔어요.

I'm Kim. **Are you going** ⁴**sightseeing today?**
저는 Kim이에요. 오늘 관광하실 건가요?

The women introduce themselves.
두 여자는 서로 소개한다.

Yes. I'd like to see Stonehenge.
네, 저는 스톤헨지를 보고 싶어요.

Ruth talks about her plans.
Ruth는 자신의 계획을 얘기한다.

That'd be great. Thanks!
그럼 좋지요. 고마워요!

I have a car. **Why don't we** go together?
제 차가 있는데, 같이 가시겠어요?

How long does it take to get there?
거기까지는 얼마나 걸릴까요?

It will take you about an hour and a half by car.
차로 한 시간 반 정도 걸릴 거예요.

Kim offers to ⁵**give Ruth a ride to Stonehenge.**
Kim은 Ruth에게 스톤헨지까지 태워주겠다고 한다.

The concierge tells them how far away it is.
안내원은 그들에게 목적지까지 거리가 얼마나 되는지 알려준다.

What are the hours?
관람 시간은 어떻게 되죠?

It opens at 9:30 a.m. and closes at 6:00 p.m.
9시 30분에 열어서 6시에 문을 닫아요.

Kim ⁶**wonders what hours Stonehenge is open.**
Kim은 스톤헨지의 관람 시간을 물어본다.

My pleasure. Enjoy your visit!
천만에요. 좋은 시간 되세요!

Thanks for your help.
도와주셔서 고맙습니다.

The women leave for Stonehenge.
두 여자는 스톤헨지로 떠난다.

MATCHING

올바른 영영 뜻을 B열에서 찾아 A열 옆에 쓰세요.

A
_____ 1. accent
_____ 2. brochure
_____ 3. give a ride
_____ 4. sightseeing
_____ 5. wonder

B
a. the way a person speaks words 억양
b. to want to know something 궁금해하다
c. to drive someone somewhere 태워주다
d. the act of going to famous or interesting places 관광
e. a small book that has information about a place or event (안내용) 책자

CONVERSATION

올바른 영어 표현으로 쓰고 말해보세요.

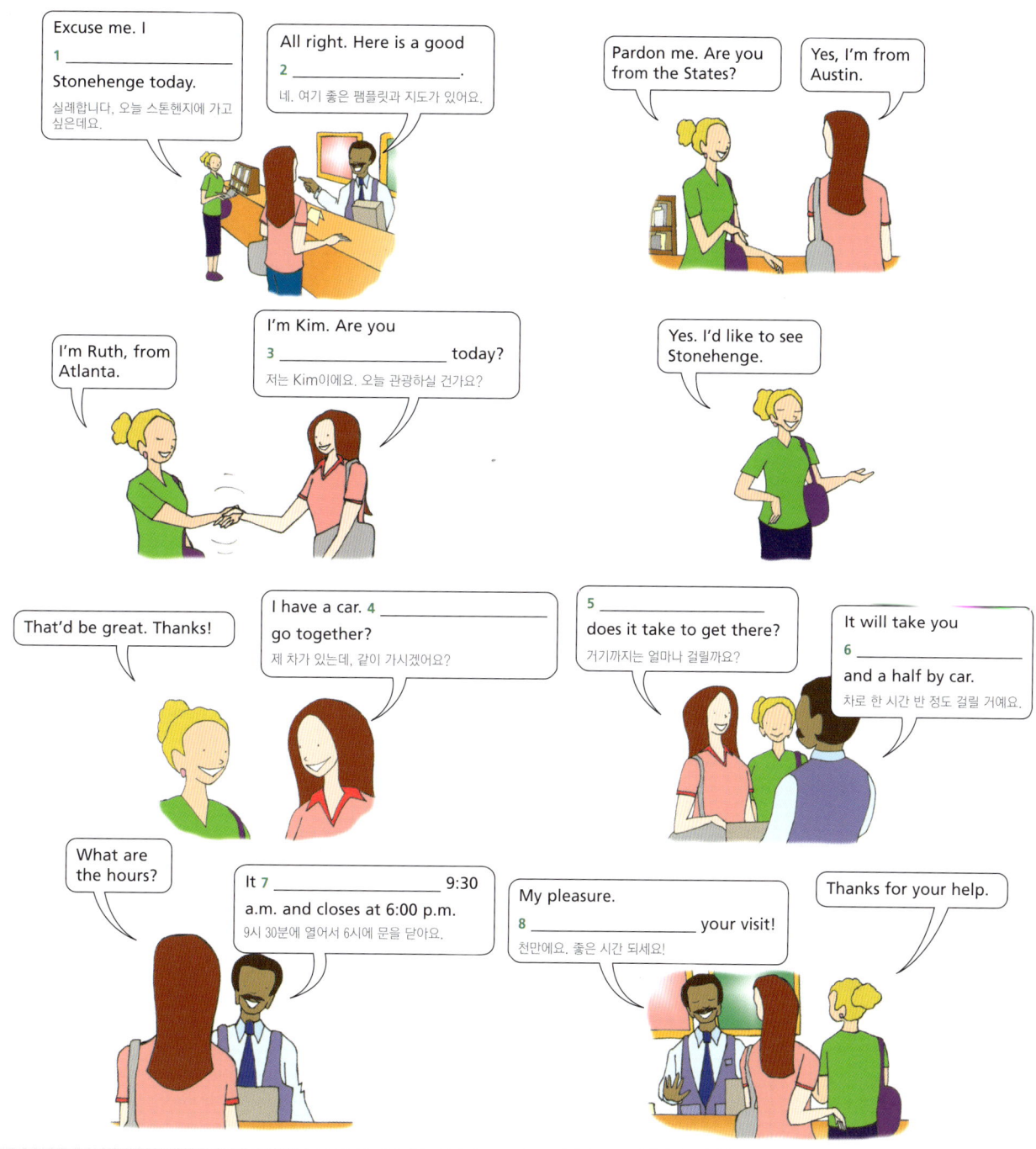

Excuse me. I 1 _____ Stonehenge today.
실례합니다, 오늘 스톤헨지에 가고 싶은데요.

All right. Here is a good 2 _____.
네, 여기 좋은 팸플릿과 지도가 있어요.

Pardon me. Are you from the States?

Yes, I'm from Austin.

I'm Ruth, from Atlanta.

I'm Kim. Are you 3 _____ today?
저는 Kim이에요. 오늘 관광하실 건가요?

Yes. I'd like to see Stonehenge.

That'd be great. Thanks!

I have a car. 4 _____ go together?
제 차가 있는데, 같이 가시겠어요?

5 _____ does it take to get there?
거기까지는 얼마나 걸릴까요?

It will take you 6 _____ and a half by car.
차로 한 시간 반 정도 걸릴 거예요.

What are the hours?

It 7 _____ 9:30 a.m. and closes at 6:00 p.m.
9시 30분에 열어서 6시에 문을 닫아요.

My pleasure. 8 _____ your visit!
천만에요. 좋은 시간 되세요!

Thanks for your help.

DAY 34
TRAVEL
관광
Sightseeing

KEY VOCABULARY

press	(버튼 등을) 누르다
button	버튼
arch	아치형 구조물
background	(사진 등의) 배경
left	왼쪽의
position	위치
smile	웃다, 미소 짓다

KEY EXPRESSIONS

- **Let's get someone to …**
  누군가에게 ~ 해달라고합시다.
  - **Let's get someone to** take our picture.
    누군가에게 사진을 찍어달라고 합시다.
  - **Let's get someone to** take our group photo.
    누군가에게 우리 단체 사진을 찍어달라고 합시다.

- **Just (동사) … ~ 하시면 됩니다.**
  - **Just** press this button.
    이 버튼을 누르시면 됩니다.
  - **Just** hold down this button for three seconds.
    이 버튼을 3초 동안 누르시면 됩니다.

- **Could you get …?**
  ~ 이 나오게 찍어 주시겠어요?
  - **Could you get** that arch in the background, please?
    저 아치형 구조물이 배경에 나오게 찍어주시겠어요?
  - **Could you get** that picture behind me as well?
    제 뒤에 있는 그림도 나오게 찍어주시겠어요?

- **Can you move …?** ~ 로 움직이시겠어요?
  - **Can you move** a bit to your left?
    조금 왼쪽으로 움직이시겠어요?
  - **Can you move** forward a little?
    앞쪽으로 조금 움직이시겠어요?

STUDY TIP

스톤헨지는 기원전 2750년경에 세 단계에 나뉘서 만들어졌을 것으로 추정된다. 돌을 의미하는 '스탄(stan)'과 돌쩌귀를 의미하는 '헹그(hencg)'라는 고대 영어 단어에서 유래한 말인 스톤헨지는 헨리 시대보다 수백 년 앞서 영국을 정복한 색슨족이 붙인 이름이다.

대화를 들어보세요. 그런 다음 롤플레잉을 해보세요.

What do you think?
어때요?

It's amazing!
대단하네요!

Ruth and Kim walk around Stonehenge.
Ruth와 Kim은 스톤헨지를 둘러본다.

Let's get someone to take our picture.
누군가에게 사진을 찍어달라고 합시다.

Good idea!
좋은 생각이네요!

Kim takes out her camera.
Kim은 카메라를 꺼낸다.

Excuse me, sir. Could you take our picture for us?
실례합니다, 선생님. 사진 좀 찍어 줄 수 있으세요?

Sure.
물론입니다.

turban
터번

Kim asks a man to take their picture.
Kim은 한 남자에게 사진 찍어 달라고 부탁한다.

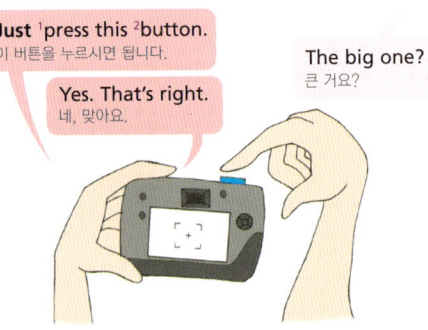

Just ¹press this ²button.
이 버튼을 누르시면 됩니다.

The big one?
큰 거요?

Yes. That's right.
네, 맞아요.

Kim shows the man how to use her camera.
Kim은 남자에게 카메라 사용법을 알려준다.

Can you get that ³arch in the ⁴background, please?
저 아치형 구조물이 배경에 나오게 찍어주시겠어요?

No problem.
문제없어요.

Kim tells the man what she wants in the picture.
Kim은 남자에게 사진에 넣고 싶은 것을 말한다.

Can you move a bit to your ⁵left?
조금 왼쪽으로 움직이시겠어요?

Is this OK?
이제 되었나요?

Perfect.
좋아요.

The women change their ⁶positions.
두 여자는 위치를 바꾼다.

OK, ⁷Smile! One, two, three…
좋아요. 웃으세요! 하나, 둘, 셋…

The man takes the picture.
남자는 사진을 찍는다.

Thank you very much!
고마워요.

You're welcome.
천만에요.

The man gives back the camera.
남자는 카메라를 돌려준다.

MATCHING

올바른 영영 뜻을 B열에서 찾아 A열 옆에 쓰세요.

A	B
_____ 1. arch	a. a small object on a machine that you push 버튼
_____ 2. background	b. to push (버튼 등을) 누르다
_____ 3. button	c. the curved part of a building or bridge 아치형 구조물
_____ 4. press	d. the space behind an object (사진 등의) 배경
_____ 5. smile	e. to make a happy face by curving your mouth up 웃다

CONVERSATION

올바른 영어 표현으로 쓰고 말해보세요.

What do you think?
It's 1 _____!
대단하네요!

Let's 2 _____ to take our picture.
누군가에게 사진을 찍어달라고 합시다.

Good idea!

Excuse me, sir. Could you 3 _____ for us?
실례합니다, 선생님. 사진 좀 찍어 줄 수 있으세요?

Sure.

Just 4 _____ this button.
이 버튼을 누르시면 됩니다.

Yes. That's right.

The big one?

Can you get that arch 5 _____, please?
저 아치형 구조물이 배경에 나오게 찍어주시겠어요?

No problem.

Can you 6 _____ to your left?
조금 왼쪽으로 움직이시겠어요?

Perfect.

Is this OK?

OK, Smile! One, two, three...

Thank you very much!

7 _____.
천만에요.

SECTION 7 TRAVEL 87

TRAVEL
DAY 35
호텔 체크아웃
Hotel Check-out

— KEY VOCABULARY

check out	(호텔 등에서 비용을 지불하고) 나가다
mini-bar	미니바
prepare	준비하다
bill	계산서
charge	(상품·서비스에 대한) 요금
explain	설명하다

— KEY EXPRESSIONS

- **I'd like to ...** ~하고 싶은데요.
  - **I'd like to** check out, please.
    체크아웃하고 싶은데요.
  - **I'd like to** extend my stay, please.
    며칠 더 머무르고 싶은데요.

- **Kim returns ...** Kim은 ~을 반납한다.
  - **Kim returns** her room key.
    Kim은 객실 키를 반납한다.
  - **Kim returns** the hair dryer.
    Kim은 헤어드라이어를 반납한다.

- **Thank you for ...** ~해서 감사합니다.
  - **Thank you for** staying with us.
    저희 호텔을 이용해 주셔서 감사합니다.
  - **Thank you for** staying at the Merchant Hill Hotel.
    머천트 힐 호텔을 이용해주셔서 감사합니다.

— STUDY TIP

체크아웃할 때 쓸 수 있는 다양한 표현:

I'm checking out now.
지금 체크아웃하려고요.

Check out, please. Room 307.
307호 체크아웃해주세요.

Can I check out now?
지금 체크아웃 할 수 있어요?

I'd like to pay my bill, please.
지금 계산하고 싶습니다.

대화를 들어보세요. 그런 다음 롤플레잉을 해보세요.

Good morning, ma'am.
안녕하세요, 손님.

Good morning. I'd like to ¹check out, please.
안녕하세요. 체크아웃하고 싶은데요.

Of course. What is your room number, please?
물론이죠. 객실 번호가 어떻게 되죠?

617. Here's my key.
617호입니다. 객실 키는 여기 있어요.

Kim puts her suitcase down.
Kim은 가방을 내려놓는다.

Kim returns her room key.
Kim은 객실 키를 반납한다.

Thank you. Did you use anything from the ²mini-bar?
감사합니다. 미니바 이용하신 것 있으세요?

No, I didn't.
아니요.

All right. Please check your bill and sign it.
다 됐습니다. 계산서를 확인하시고 서명해 주세요.

The receptionist ³prepares Kim's ⁴bill.
접수 담당자는 Kim의 계산서를 준비한다.

The receptionist hands Kim the bill and a pen.
접수 담당자는 Kim에게 계산서와 펜을 준다.

Excuse me, what is this ⁵charge here?
실례하지만, 여기 이 요금은 무엇에 대한 거죠?

That is for a call from your room.
그건 객실에서 사용하신 전화 요금입니다.

Oh, yes. I called the airport.
아, 맞아요. 공항에 전화를 걸었어요.

Kim points to a part of the bill.
Kim은 계산서 한 부분을 가리킨다.

The receptionist ⁶explains the charge.
접수 담당자는 요금에 대해 설명한다.

Everything looks OK then.
그럼 이제 모든 것이 된 것 같군요.

All right. Here is your receipt.
좋습니다. 여기 영수증 받으세요.

Thank you for staying with us, Miss Jones. Have a nice day.
저희 호텔을 이용해 주셔서 감사합니다. Jones씨. 좋은 하루 되세요.

Thank you very much. Good-bye!
감사합니다. 안녕히 계세요!

The receptionist gives Kim her receipt.
접수 담당자는 Kim에게 영수증을 건넨다.

Kim picks up her bags and leaves.
Kim은 가방을 들고 떠난다.

MATCHING

올바른 영영 뜻을 B열에서 찾아 A열 옆에 쓰세요.

A
1. bill
2. charge
3. explain
4. mini-bar
5. prepare

B
a. the cost of an item or service (상품서비스에 대한) 요금
b. a small fridge in a hotel room with drinks inside 미니바
c. to get ready 준비하다
d. a piece of paper that shows how much you must pay 계산서
e. to help someone understand something 설명하다

CONVERSATION

올바른 영어 표현으로 쓰고 말해보세요.

SECTION 8

Health

건강 챙기기

Scan for Preview

DAY 36 Exercise
운동

DAY 37 An Accident
사고

DAY 38 In the Doctor's Office
병원에서

DAY 39 The Examination
진찰

DAY 40 At the Pharmacy
약국에서

HEALTH
DAY 36
운동
Exercise

KEY VOCABULARY

glad (syn. happy, pleased)	기쁜
exercise	운동하다
work out	운동하다
rollerblade	롤러블레이드
outdoors (ant. indoors)	야외에서
gym	체육관
take off	벗다
volleyball	배구
basketball	농구
ski	스키를 타다
lock (syn. fasten)	잠그다

KEY EXPRESSIONS

- **How often do you …?**
  얼마나 자주 ~ 하세요?
  - **How often do you** exercise?
    얼마나 자주 운동하세요?
  - **How often do you** go to the gym?
    얼마나 자주 체육관에 가세요?

- **I try to …** ~ 하려고 해요.
  - **I try to** work out three times a week.
    1주일에 3번 정도 운동하려고 해요.
  - **I try to** go every other day.
    하루걸러 하려고 해요.

- **That's why …** 그래서 ~ 해요.
  - **That's why** I like rollerblading.
    그래서 롤러블레이드 타는 걸 좋아하나 봐요.
  - **That's why** I left so early.
    그래서 제가 그렇게 일찍 나왔어요.

- **How long have you been …?**
  얼마나 ~ 하셨어요?
  - **How long have you been** rollerblading?
    롤러블레이드를 얼마나 타셨어요?
  - **How long have you been** weightlifting?
    역도를 얼마나 하셨어요?

STUDY TIP

few, a few, little, a little의 차이:

few와 little은 셀 수 있냐 없냐의 차이다.
또한 a가 붙으면 긍정의 뜻이 되고 a가 붙지 않은 경우 부정의 뜻이 된다.

뜻	셀 수 있음	셀 수 없음
약간의	a few	a little
거의 없는 (부정)	few	little

대화를 들어보세요. 그런 다음 롤플레잉을 해보세요.

Kim and Mary go to the park to ²exercise.
Kim과 Mary는 공원으로 운동하러 간다.

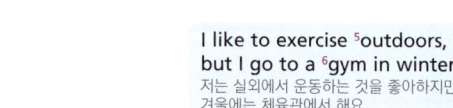

They take out their bags.
그들은 가방을 꺼낸다.

Kim puts on her ⁴rollerblades.
Kim은 롤러블레이드를 신는다.

Mary sits down and ⁷takes off her shoes.
Mary는 앉아서 신발을 벗는다.

Mary puts on her pads.
Mary는 보호대를 착용한다.

They put their shoes in their bags.
그들은 신발을 가방에 넣는다.

They ¹¹lock their bags in the car.
그들은 가방을 차에 넣고 차 문을 잠근다.

Kim and Mary put on their helmets and start to rollerblade.
Kim과 Mary는 헬멧을 쓰고 롤러블레이드를 타기 시작한다.

MATCHING

올바른 영영 뜻을 B열에서 찾아 A열 옆에 쓰세요.

A

_____ 1. basketball
_____ 2. glad
_____ 3. outdoors
_____ 4. volleyball
_____ 5. work out

B

a. not inside 야외에서
b. happy 기쁜
c. to exercise 운동하다
d. a sport played by hitting a ball with your hands 배구
e. a sport played by throwing a ball into a hoop 농구

CONVERSATION

올바른 영어 표현으로 쓰고 말해보세요.

I'm glad we could
1 _____!
함께 하게 돼 기뻐요!

Me, too.

2 _____
do you exercise?
얼마나 자주 운동하세요?

I try to work out
3 _____.
1주일에 3번 정도 운동하려고 해요.

Where do you go?

I like to exercise outdoors, but I
4 _____ in winter.
저는 실외에서 운동하는 것을 좋아하지만, 겨울에는 체육관에서 해요.

What sports 5 _____?
어떤 운동을 좋아하세요?

I like volleyball and basketball.

How about you?

I like to ski.
6 _____
I like rollerblading.
저는 스키 타기를 좋아해요.
그래서 롤러블레이드 타는 걸 좋아하나 봐요.

7 _____
have you been rollerblading?
롤러블레이드를 타기 시작한 지는 얼마나 되셨어요?

Just a few months.

Well, are you ready?

Sure, let's go!

HEALTH

DAY 37

사고
An Accident

■ KEY VOCABULARY

fall	넘어지다, 쓰러지다
backward	뒤의
happen	발생하다, 벌어지다
balance	균형, 평형
kneel down	무릎을 꿇고 앉다
beside (syn. next to)	옆에
sprain	삐다, 접질리다
wrist	손목, 팔목
skate	스케이트를 타다
curb	(차도 가의) 연석

■ KEY EXPRESSIONS

- **I think I …** ~ 한 것 같아요.
  - **I think I** sprained my wrist! 손목을 삔 것 같아요!
  - **I think I** twisted my ankle. 발목을 삔 것 같아요.

- **Can you move …?** ~을 움직일 수 있겠어요?
  - **Can you move** it at all? 움직일 수 있겠어요?
  - **Can you move** your foot? 발을 움직일 수 있겠어요?

- **I don't think …** ~ 것 같지는 않아요.
  - **I don't think** it's broken. 부러진 것 같지는 않아요.
  - **I don't think** it's sprained. 삔 것 같지는 않아요.

- **I'll get …** ~을 가져올게요.
  - **I'll get** your bag. 가방을 가져올게요.
  - **I'll get** your phone. 당신의 전화기를 가져올게요.

■ STUDY TIP

다양한 신체 부위:
ankle 발목
backbone 척추
breast 가슴
chest 흉부
heel 발뒤꿈치
hip 엉덩이
waist 허리

대화를 들어보세요. 그런 다음 롤플레잉을 해보세요.

Ouch!
아이쿠!

Mary ¹falls ²backwards.
Mary는 뒤로 넘어진다.

Mary! Are you OK?
Mary! 괜찮아요?

Kim turns back to see Mary.
Kim은 뒤로 돌아 Mary를 본다.

What ³happened?
어떻게 된 거예요?

I lost my ⁴balance.
균형을 잃었어요.

Kim ⁵kneels down ⁶beside Mary.
Kim은 Mary 옆에 무릎을 꿇고 앉는다.

I think I ⁷sprained my ⁸wrist!
손목을 삔 것 같아요!

Are you hurt?
다쳤어요?

Kim checks on Mary.
Kim은 Mary를 살펴본다.

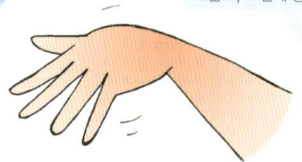

Can you move it at all?
손목을 움직일 수 있겠어요?

A little bit, but it hurts.
조금요, 그런데 통증이 있어요.

Mary tries to move her wrist.
Mary는 손목을 움직여보려고 한다.

Well, I don't think it's broken.
글쎄, 부러진 것 같지는 않아요.

Kim helps Mary stand up.
Kim은 Mary를 부축해 일으켜 세운다.

Let's go home and put some ice on it.
집으로 가서 얼음찜질합시다.

What should I do?
어떻게 해야지?

Kim helps Mary ⁹skate back to the car.
Kim은 Mary가 스케이트를 타고 차로 돌아가는 것을 돕는다.

Sit down. I'll get your bag. Can I have the keys?
앉아 있어요. 가방 가져올게요. 열쇠 주실래요?

Here you go. Thanks, Kim.
여기요. 고마워요, Kim.

Mary sits on the ¹⁰curb and gives Kim the car keys.
Mary는 연석에 앉아 Kim에게 자동차 열쇠를 준다.

MATCHING

올바른 영영 뜻을 B열에서 찾아 A열 옆에 쓰세요.

A	B
___ 1. balance	a. next to 옆에
___ 2. beside	b. to move using skates 스케이트를 타다
___ 3. curb	c. the place where your hand joins your arm 손목, 팔목
___ 4. skate	d. the state of standing without falling to one side 균형
___ 5. wrist	e. the edge where a sidewalk meets a road (차도 가의) 연석

CONVERSATION

올바른 영어 표현으로 쓰고 말해보세요.

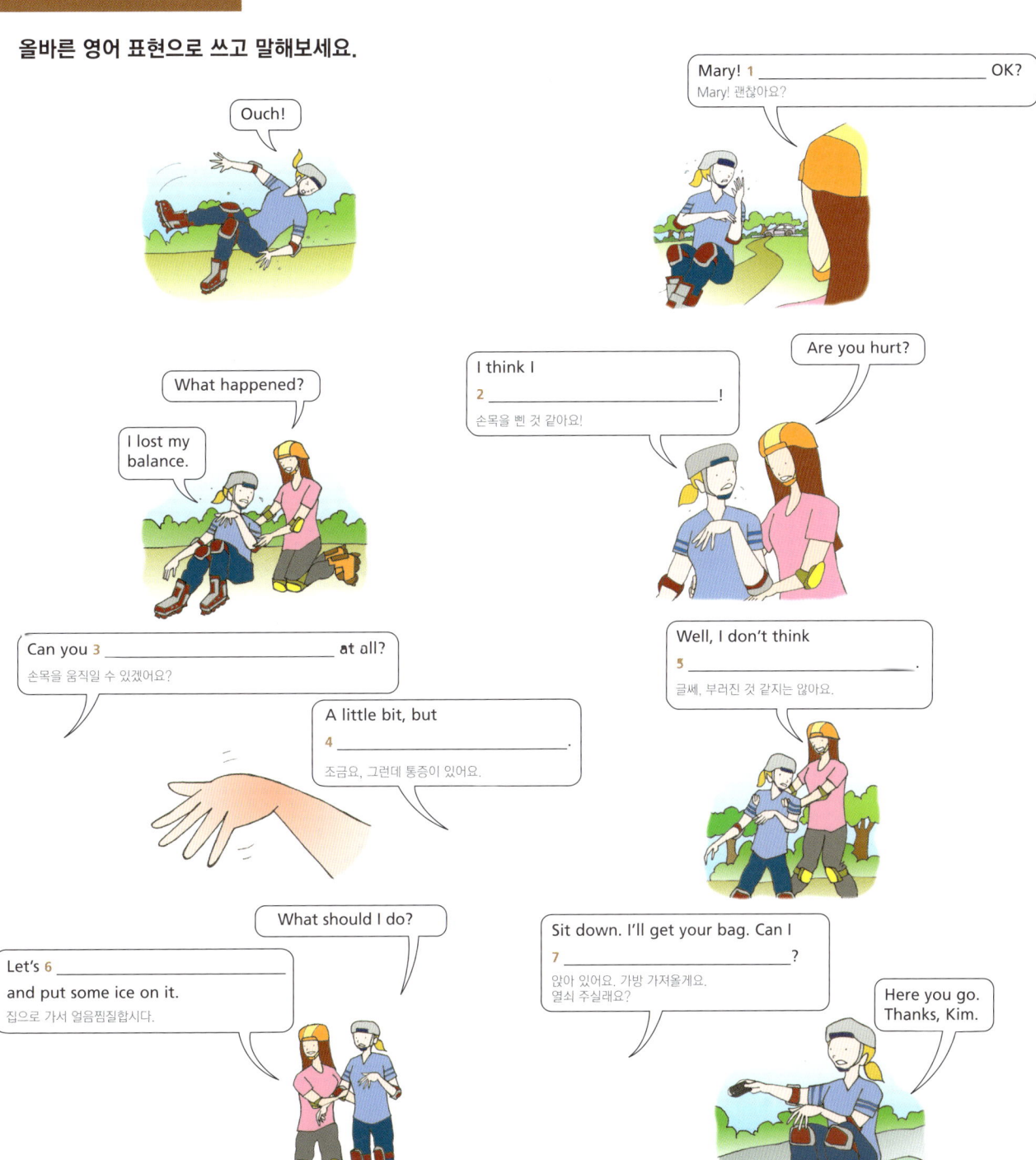

Mary! 1 _____ OK?
Mary! 괜찮아요?

Ouch!

Are you hurt?

What happened?

I think I
2 _____!
손목을 삔 것 같아요!

I lost my balance.

Can you 3 _____ at all?
손목을 움직일 수 있겠어요?

Well, I don't think
5 _____.
글쎄, 부러진 것 같지는 않아요.

A little bit, but
4 _____.
조금요, 그런데 통증이 있어요.

What should I do?

Sit down. I'll get your bag. Can I
7 _____?
앉아 있어요. 가방 가져올게요.
열쇠 주실래요?

Let's 6 _____
and put some ice on it.
집으로 가서 얼음찜질합시다.

Here you go.
Thanks, Kim.

HEALTH
DAY 38
병원에서
In the Doctor's Office

━ KEY VOCABULARY

appointment	약속, 예약
reception desk	접수처
insurance card	건강보험 카드
direct	~로 향하다
waiting area	대기실
recognize (syn. notice)	알아보다, 알다
cold	감기
nurse	간호사
patient	환자
examination room	진찰실

━ KEY EXPRESSIONS

- **May I see …?** ~를 보여주시겠어요?
  - **May I see** your insurance card, please**?**
    건강보험 카드를 보여주시겠어요?
  - **May I see** your ID**?**
    신분증을 보여주시겠어요?

- **… hand over …**
  ~가 ~을 건네다.
  - Mary **hands over** her insurance card.
    Mary는 건강보험 카드를 건넨다.
  - The nurse **hands over** a form.
    간호사가 양식을 건넨다.

- **… point to …** ~가 ~을 가리키다.
  - The nurse **points to** the examination room.
    간호사가 진찰실을 가리킨다.
  - The nurse **points to** the machine.
    간호사가 기계를 가리킨다.

━ STUDY TIP

병원에서 사용할 수 있는 표현:

I have a fever.
열이 있어요.

I have a runny nose.
콧물이 나요.

I have the flu.
독감에 걸렸어요.

My body aches all over.
온몸이 몸살 난 것처럼 쑤셔요.

I have a sore throat.
목이 아파요.

대화를 들어보세요. 그런 다음 롤플레잉을 해보세요.

Good afternoon. How may I help you?
안녕하세요. 무엇을 도와드릴까요?

Hello. I'm Mary Smith. I have an ¹appointment at 2:30.
안녕하세요. 저는 Mary Smith인데, 2시 30분으로 예약했어요.

Mary goes to the ²reception desk at the doctor's office.
Mary는 병원 접수대로 간다.

May I see your ³insurance card, please?
건강보험 카드를 보여주실래요?

Here you are.
여기 있습니다.

Mary **hands over** her insurance card.
Mary는 건강보험 카드를 건넨다.

All right. Please have a seat. The doctor will see you soon.
좋아요, 앉아서 기다리시면, 의사 선생님께서 곧 보실 거예요.

The receptionist ⁴directs Mary to the ⁵waiting area.
접수원이 Mary에게 대기실에 가 있도록 한다.

Hi, Mary.
안녕, 메리.

Carlos! Why are you here?
Carlos! 여긴 어쩐 일이세요?

Mary ⁶recognizes someone in the waiting room.
Mary는 대기실에서 누군가를 알아본다.

I have a really bad ⁷cold. How about you?
지독한 감기에 걸렸어요. 당신은 웬일이에요?

I fell down and hurt my wrist.
넘어져서 손목을 다쳤어요.

Carlos Lopez, the doctor will see you now.
Carlos Lopez씨, 진료받을 차례입니다.

Mary sits down next to Carlos.
Mary는 Carlos 옆에 앉는다.

The ⁸nurse calls the next ⁹patient.
간호사가 다음 환자를 부른다.

Well, I hope you feel better, Mary.
쾌유를 빌어요, Mary.

You too, Carlos.
당신도요, Carlos.

Carlos follows the nurse to the ¹⁰examination room.
Carlos는 간호사를 따라 진찰실로 간다.

Please sit here. Dr. Graham will be with you soon.
여기 앉으세요. Graham 박사님께서 곧 오실 거예요.

Thanks.
고마워요.

stethoscope
청진기

The nurse **points to** the examination room.
간호사는 진찰실을 가리킨다.

MATCHING

올바른 영영 뜻을 B열에서 찾아 A열 옆에 쓰세요.

A	B
___ 1. appointment	a. a room in a hospital where a doctor treats you 진찰실
___ 2. examination room	b. a sick or hurt person in a hospital 환자
___ 3. nurse	c. a hospital worker who takes care of sick people 간호사
___ 4. patient	d. a room you sit in a while waiting for something 대기실
___ 5. waiting room	e. an agreement to meet at a certain time 예약

CONVERSATION

올바른 영어 표현으로 쓰고 말해보세요.

Good afternoon. How may I help you?

Hello. I'm Mary Smith. I 1 _____ at 2:30.
안녕하세요. 저는 Mary Smith인데, 2시 30분으로 예약했어요.

May I see your 2 _____, please?
건강보험 카드를 보여주실래요?

Here you are.

All right. Please 3 _____.
The doctor will see you soon.
좋아요, 앉아서 기다리시면, 의사 선생님께서 곧 보실 거예요.

Hi, Mary.

Carlos! Why are you here?

I have a 4 _____.
How about you?
지독한 감기에 걸렸어요. 당신은 웬일이에요?

I 5 _____ and hurt my wrist.
넘어져서 손목을 다쳤어요.

Carlos Lopez, the doctor will see you now.

Well, I hope you 6 _____, Mary.
쾌유를 빌어요, Mary.

You too, Carlos.

Please 7 _____.
Dr. Graham will be with you soon.
여기 앉으세요. Graham 박사님께서 곧 오실 거예요.

Thanks.

SECTION 8 HEALTH 97

DAY 39

HEALTH

진찰
The Examination

▬ KEY VOCABULARY

trouble	병, 통증, 문제
glove	장갑
cough	기침하다
all the time	내내, 줄곧
throat	목구멍, 목
sore (syn. painful)	아픈, 따가운, 화끈거리는
swollen	부어오른
breathe	호흡하다, 숨을 쉬다
deeply	깊이
infection	감염
medicine	약, 약물
serious (syn. critical)	심각한
prescription	처방전
rest (syn. relax)	쉬다, 휴식을 취하다
plenty of	많은
fluid	액체

▬ KEY EXPRESSIONS

- **I have …** (병명) ~에 걸린 것 같아요.
  - **I have** a very bad cold.
    심한 감기에 걸린 것 같아요.
  - **I have** a sinus infection.
    축농증이 생긴 것 같아요.

- **… look into …** ~가 ~을 들여다보다.
  - Dr. Graham **looks into** Carlos's mouth.
    Graham 박사는 Carlos의 입을 들여다본다.
  - The nurse **looks into** Jeremy's ears.
    간호사가 Jeremy의 귀를 들여다본다.

- **You need to …** ~를 하셔야겠어요.
  - **You need to** take some medicine.
    약을 좀 드셔야겠어요.
  - **You need to** clean your ears.
    귀를 좀 파셔야겠어요.

▬ STUDY TIP

무슨 문제가 있냐고 물을 때 쓸 수 있는 표현:

What's the trouble?
What's wrong?
What seems to be the problem?
What's the matter?

대화를 들어보세요. 그런 다음 롤플레잉을 해보세요.

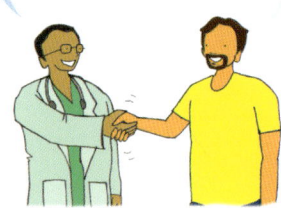

Good afternoon, Carlos.
안녕하세요, Carlos.

Hi, Dr. Graham.
안녕하세요, Graham 박사님.

They shake hands.
그들은 악수한다.

So, what's the ¹trouble today?
그런데, 오늘 어디가 편찮으시죠?

Dr. Graham puts on some ²gloves.
Graham 박사는 장갑을 낀다.

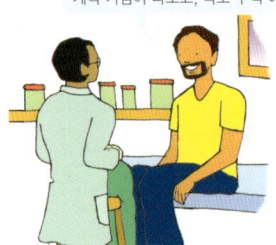

I have a very bad cold. I ³cough ⁴all the time and my ⁵throat is very ⁶sore.
저는 감기가 매우 심한 것 같아요.
계속 기침이 나오고, 목도 무척 아파요.

The doctor sits in front of Carlos.
박사는 Carlos 앞에 앉는다.

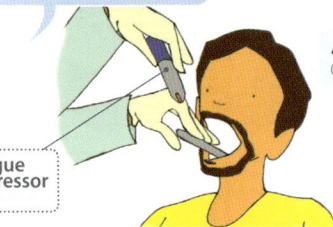

I see. Please open your mouth.
알겠습니다. 입을 벌려 보세요.

Ahhhhh…
아아아아…

tongue depressor
설압자

Dr. Graham looks into Carlos's mouth.
Graham 박사는 Carlos의 입을 들여다본다.

Your throat is very red and ⁷swollen.
목이 무척 빨갛게 부어 있군요.

The doctor puts on his stethoscope.
의사는 청진기를 착용한다.

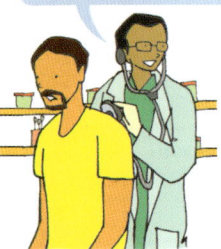

OK. Now ⁸breathe ⁹deeply.
좋아요. 이제, 숨을 깊이 쉬세요.

Carlos breathes deeply in and out.
Carlos는 숨을 깊이 들이쉬고 내쉰다.

Mmm… You have an ¹⁰infection. You need to take some ¹¹medicine.
으…음. 감염된 것 같군요. 약을 좀 드셔야겠어요.

Is it ¹²serious?
심각한가요?

Dr. Graham writes a ¹³prescription.
Graham 박사는 처방전을 작성한다.

No. Just ¹⁴rest and drink ¹⁵plenty of ¹⁶fluids.
아니에요. 쉬면서 물을 많이 드시면 괜찮을 것 같아요.

Thank you, Dr. Graham.
고맙습니다. Graham 박사님.

Carlos takes the prescription.
Carlos는 처방전을 받는다.

MATCHING

올바른 영영 뜻을 B열에서 찾아 A열 옆에 쓰세요.

A	B
_____ 1. breathe	a. a lot of; many 많은
_____ 2. fluid	b. painful; uncomfortable 아픈
_____ 3. plenty of	c. a problem 병, 통증, 문제
_____ 4. sore	d. to take air into the lungs 호흡하다
_____ 5. trouble	e. liquids, such as water 액체

CONVERSATION

올바른 영어 표현으로 쓰고 말해보세요.

Good afternoon, Carlos.

Hi, Dr. Graham.

So, 1 _____ today?
그런데, 오늘 어디가 편찮으시죠?

2 _____. I cough all the time and my throat is very sore.
저는 감기가 매우 심한 것 같아요.
계속 기침이 나오고, 목도 무척 아파요.

I see. 3 _____.
알겠습니다. 입을 벌려 보세요.

Ahhhhh...

Your throat is very red and swollen.

OK. Now 4 _____.
좋아요. 이제, 숨을 깊이 쉬세요.

Mmm... You have an infection. You 5 _____.
으...음, 감염된 것 같군요. 약을 좀 드셔야겠어요.

Is it serious?

No. Just rest and drink 6 _____.
아니에요. 쉬면서 물을 많이 드시면 괜찮을 것 같아요.

Thank you, Dr. Graham.

HEALTH
DAY 40
약국에서
At the Pharmacy

━ KEY VOCABULARY

pharmacist (syn. chemist)	약사
have a seat	자리에 앉다
dosage	(보통 약의) 복용량, 투여량
paper bag	종이봉투
side effect	(약의) 부작용
dizziness	현기증, 어지러움
upset stomach	복통, 배탈
cough drop	(기침을 멎게 하는) 알약
soothe	(통증 등을) 누그러뜨리다

━ KEY EXPRESSIONS

- **I'd like to get ...** ~을 받고 싶습니다.
  - **I'd like to get** this prescription filled.
    이 처방전의 약을 받고 싶습니다.
  - **I'd like to get** a new pair of lenses.
    새로운 렌즈 한 쌍을 받고 싶습니다.

- **... wait for ...** ~는 ~을 기다리다.
  - Carlos **waits for** his prescription.
    Carlos는 처방전 약을 기다린다.
  - Connie **waits for** his doctor.
    Connie는 의사를 기다린다.

- **You should take ...** ~를 드세요.
  - **You should take** one pill three times a day.
    한 번에 한 알씩 하루 세 번 드세요.
  - **You should take** these pills three times a day.
    이 알약들을 하루에 세 번 드세요.

- **You may have some ...**
  ~가 있을 수도 있어요.
  - **You may have some** dizziness or an upset stomach.
    현기증이나 위통이 있을 수도 있어요.
  - **You may have some** nausea.
    메스꺼울 수도 있어요.

━ STUDY TIP

다른 부작용(side effects)에는 fatigue(피로감), muscle pain(근육통), mild fever(미열), arm pain(팔 통증), skin rash(두드러기), drowsiness(졸음) 등이 있다.

대화를 들어보세요. 그런 다음 롤플레잉을 해보세요.

Carlos hands his prescription to the ¹pharmacist.
Carlos는 처방전을 약사에게 건넨다.

Carlos **waits for** his prescription.
Carlos는 처방전 약을 기다린다.

The pharmacist brings a bottle of pills to the counter.
약사는 알약 한 병을 카운터에 올려놓는다.

Carlos asks about the ³dosage.
Carlos는 복용량에 대해 질문한다.

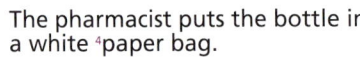

The pharmacist puts the bottle in a white ⁴paper bag.
약사는 병을 하얀 종이봉투에 넣는다.

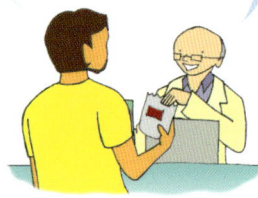

The pharmacist gives Carlos the medicine.
약사는 Carlos에게 약을 건넨다.

Carlos asks about other medicine.
Carlos는 다른 약에 대해 물어본다.

The pharmacist hands Carlos a pack of cough drops.
약사는 Carlos에게 기침약 한 갑을 건넨다.

MATCHING

올바른 영영 뜻을 B열에서 찾아 A열 옆에 쓰세요.

A	B
_____ 1. cough drop	a. the amount of medicine you have to take (보통 약의) 복용량
_____ 2. dosage	b. a worker who gives out medicine 약사
_____ 3. have a seat	c. to sit down 자리에 앉다
_____ 4. pharmacist	d. a small tablet, often sweet that treats a cough (기침을 멎게 하는) 알약
_____ 5. upset stomach	e. pain in the stomach 배탈

CONVERSATION

올바른 영어 표현으로 쓰고 말해보세요.

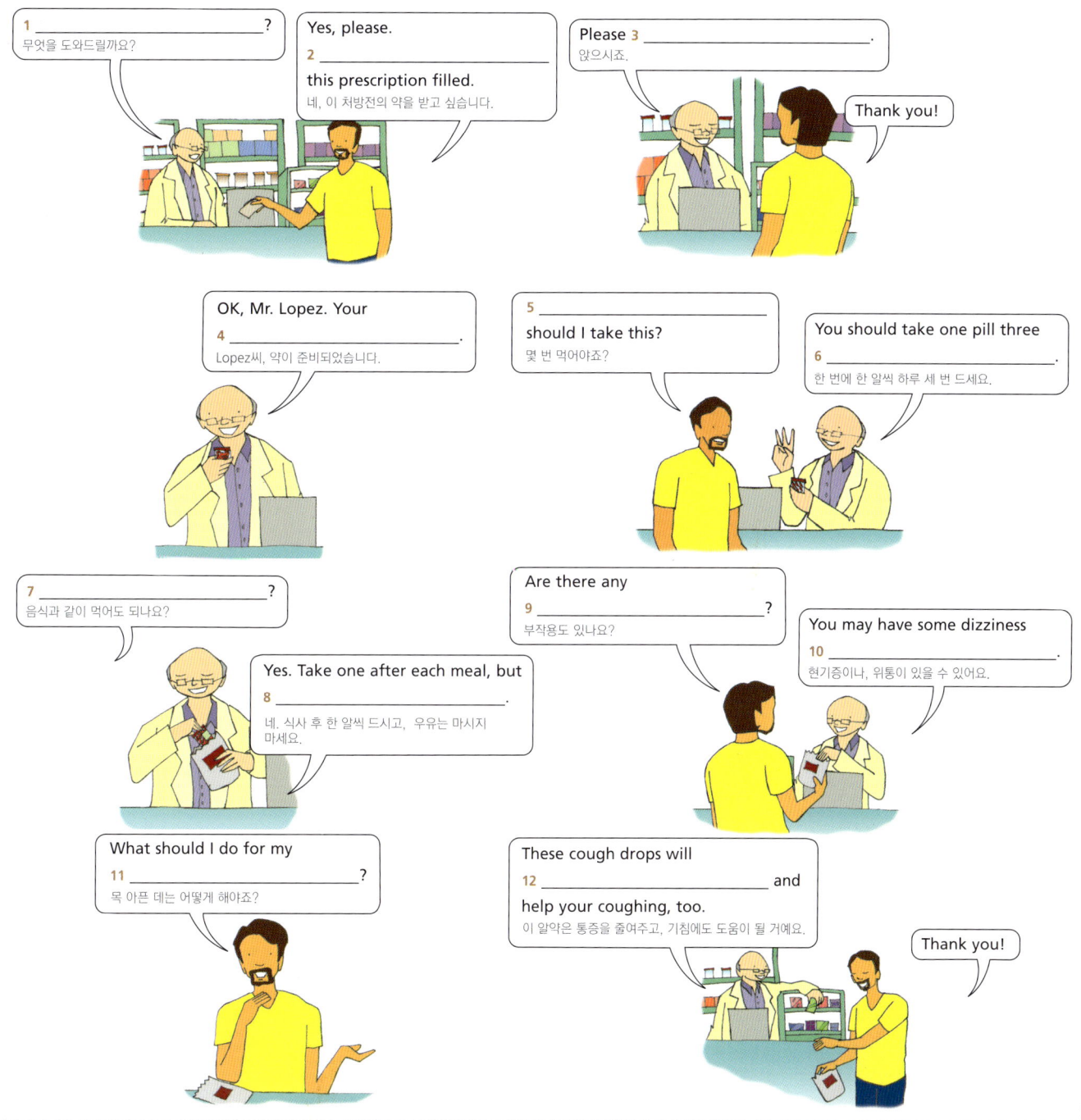

1 _____? 무엇을 도와드릴까요?

Yes, please. 2 _____ this prescription filled. 네, 이 처방전의 약을 받고 싶습니다.

Please 3 _____. 앉으시죠.

Thank you!

OK, Mr. Lopez. Your 4 _____. Lopez씨, 약이 준비되었습니다.

5 _____ should I take this? 몇 번 먹어야죠?

You should take one pill three 6 _____. 한 번에 한 알씩 하루 세 번 드세요.

7 _____? 음식과 같이 먹어도 되나요?

Yes. Take one after each meal, but 8 _____. 네, 식사 후 한 알씩 드시고, 우유는 마시지 마세요.

Are there any 9 _____? 부작용도 있나요?

You may have some dizziness 10 _____. 현기증이나, 위통이 있을 수 있어요.

What should I do for my 11 _____? 목 아픈 데는 어떻게 해야죠?

These cough drops will 12 _____ and help your coughing, too. 이 알약은 통증을 줄여주고, 기침에도 도움이 될 거예요.

Thank you!

SECTION 9

Special Occasions

특별한 날

| DAY **41** | **Planning a Party**
파티 계획 짜기

| DAY **42** | **Other Plans**
다른 계획

| DAY **43** | **Party Preparation**
파티 준비

| DAY **44** | **Wrapping a Gift**
선물 포장하기

| DAY **45** | **At the Party**
파티에서

SPECIAL OCCASIONS

DAY 41

파티 계획 짜기
Planning a Party

▬ KEY VOCABULARY

class (syn. course)	수업, 강좌
gather	(여기저기 있는 것을) 모으다
have a party	파티를 열다
slip	(옷 등을) 재빨리 입다, 걸치다
classroom	교실
chicken tortillas	닭고기 토르티야
cake	케이크
bake	(음식을) 굽다

▬ KEY EXPRESSIONS

- **Do you have plans …?**
  ~ 에 계획이 있나요?
  - **Do you have plans** next Friday?
    다음 금요일에 계획이 있나요?
  - **Do you have plans** this weekend?
    이번 주말에 계획이 있나요?

- **I want to have …** ~ 을 하고 싶어요.
  - **I want to have** a party for her at our house.
    우리 집에서 그녀를 위한 파티를 열고 싶어요.
  - **I want to have** a little dinner for my parents.
    부모님을 위한 간단한 저녁 식사를 준비하고 싶어요.

- **I'll make …** ~ 를 만들게요.
  - **I'll make** my chicken tortillas!
    닭고기 토르티야를 만들게요!
  - **I'll make** some cookies.
    쿠키를 좀 만들게요.

- **… decide to …** ~ 가 ~ 하기로 하다.
  - Mary **decides to** make a cake.
    Mary는 케이크를 만들기로 한다.
  - Martha **decides to** make a pie.
    Martha는 파이를 만들기로 한다.

▬ STUDY TIP

미국에서는 모임에 참석하는 사람들이 각자 한 가지의 음식을 만들어 가지고 와서 나눠 먹는 파티 문화가 발달해있다. 미국뿐 아니라 캐나다에서도 이어져 오는 전통으로 이를 'potluck'이라고 한다.

대화를 들어보세요. 그런 다음 롤플레잉을 해보세요.

Mary and Julia talk after class.
Mary와 Julia는 수업 후에 이야기를 나눈다.

They ²gather their books.
그들은 책을 챙긴다.

Mary ⁴slips her bag over her shoulder.
Mary는 가방을 어깨에 걸친다.

Julia puts her books in her bag.
Julia는 책을 가방에 넣는다.

They agree on the time.
그들은 시간을 정한다.

They walk out of the ⁵classroom.
그들은 강의실에서 걸어 나온다.

Julia offers to make a special dish.
Julia는 특별요리를 만들겠다고 제안한다.

Mary decides to make a cake.
Mary는 케이크를 만들기로 한다.

MATCHING

올바른 영영 뜻을 B열에서 찾아 A열 옆에 쓰세요.

A	B
___ 1. bake	a. to cook something in an oven (음식을) 굽다
___ 2. cake	b. a lesson given by a teacher 수업
___ 3. class	c. a baked food made with flour, eggs, and sugar 케이크
___ 4. classroom	d. to collect (여기저기 있는 것을) 모으다
___ 5. gather	e. a room that students study in 교실

CONVERSATION

올바른 영어 표현으로 쓰고 말해보세요.

SPECIAL OCCASIONS
DAY 42

다른 계획
Other Plans

▬ KEY VOCABULARY

vending machine	자동판매기, 자판기
wallet	지갑
coin	동전
slot	(가느다란) 구멍
out of town	시외로, 도시 밖으로
gift (syn. present)	선물
pass along	전달하다
congratulations	축하
mention	말하다, 언급하다

▬ KEY EXPRESSIONS

- **Did you hear about …?**
  ~ 에 대해 들었어요?
  - **Did you hear about** Kim's birthday **party?**
    Kim의 생일파티에 대해 들었어요?
  - **Did you hear about** Tony's graduation**?**
    토니의 졸업식에 대해 들었어요?

- **I have to go …** ~ 에 가야 해요.
  - **I have to go** out of town on business.
    업무차 시외로 나가야 해요.
  - **I have to go** on a trip to Maryland.
    메릴랜드로 여행을 가야 해요.

- **… give … to …** ~ 에게 ~ 를 건네다.
  - John **gives** a can **to** Carlos.
    John은 Carlos에게 캔을 건넨다.
  - Sarah **gave** a glass **to** Michael.
    Sarah는 Michael에게 병을 건넸다.

- **Good luck with …**
  ~ 잘하세요.
  - **Good luck with** your trip.
    출장 잘 다녀오세요.
  - **Good luck with** your party.
    파티 잘하시길 바랍니다.

▬ STUDY TIP

'Don't mention it.'은 직역하면 '그것에 대해 말하지 마.'로 해석되지만, 절대 그런 뜻으로 사용되지 않는다.
오히려 고맙다고 말하는 상대방에게 정중하게 '별말씀을요.'라고 하는 대답으로 쓰인다.
보통 사용하는 'You're welcome.' 대신 사용할 수 있는 표현이다.

대화를 들어보세요. 그런 다음 롤플레잉을 해보세요.

Sure, I'll take a cola. Thanks.
그러죠. 콜라 마실게요. 고마워요.

Would you like a drink?
한 잔 드시겠어요?

John and Carlos meet by the ¹vending machine.
John과 Carlos는 자동판매기 옆에서 만난다.

Did you hear about Kim's birthday party?
Kim의 생일파티에 대해 들었어요?

Yes. Julia told me about it.
네. Julia가 나에게 얘기해 주었어요.

Carlos takes money from his ²wallet.
Carlos는 지갑에서 돈을 꺼낸다.

Really? That's too bad.
그래요? 안됐군요.

However, I can't make it.
그런데, 나는 갈 수가 없네요.

He puts a ³coin into the ⁴slot.
그는 동전을 투입구에 넣는다.

Yeah, I have to go ⁵out of town on business. I'm sorry.
그래요. 업무차 시외로 나가야 해요. 안타깝네요.

Carlos pushes the button.
Carlos는 버튼을 누른다.

Don't worry about it!
걱정 마세요!

John reaches for the cans.
John은 캔을 꺼내려고 팔을 뻗는다.

We got a ⁶gift for Kim. I told Julia to wish her happy birthday for me.
우리는 Kim의 선물을 준비했어요. Julia에게 나 대신 생일 축하해 주라고 말해 놓았어요.

Carlos wants to ⁷pass along his ⁸congratulations.
Carlos는 대신 축하해 주기를 바란다.

We should get together another time.
다음에 함께 만나기로 하죠.

That would be great!
좋아요!

John **gives** a can **to** Carlos.
John은 Carlos에게 캔을 건넨다.

Good luck with your trip. Thanks for the drink.
출장 잘 다녀오세요. 고맙게 마실게요.

Don't ⁹mention it.
천만에요.

They open their drinks.
그들은 음료 뚜껑을 연다.

MATCHING

올바른 영영 뜻을 B열에서 찾아 A열 옆에 쓰세요.

A

____ 1. coin
____ 2. mention
____ 3. out of town
____ 4. vending machine
____ 5. wallet

B

a. to say 말하다, 언급하다
b. a small case that holds money 지갑
c. a round piece of metal that is used as money 동전
d. being in another city 시외로
e. a machine you can buy snacks and drinks from 자동판매기

CONVERSATION

올바른 영어 표현으로 쓰고 말해보세요.

SPECIAL OCCASIONS
DAY 43
파티 준비
Party Preparation

■ KEY VOCABULARY

decoration	(특별한 행사를 위한) 장식품
balloon	풍선
birthday banner	생일 배너
dining room	주방, 식당(방)
mixed nuts	여러 가지 견과류
cracker	크래커
tie	(끈 등으로) 묶다, 묶어 두다
string	끈, 줄
ceiling	천장
decorate	장식하다, 꾸미다

■ KEY EXPRESSIONS

- **Did you bring …?** ~을 가져왔나요?
  - **Did you bring** decorations**?** 장식할 거 가지고 왔나요?
  - **Did you bring** a present**?** 선물을 가져왔나요?

- **I brought …** ~을 가져왔어요.
  - **I brought** some balloons and a birthday banner. 풍선과 생일 배너를 가져왔어요.
  - **I brought** some dip. 찍어 먹을 소스를 좀 가져왔어요.

- **… be preparing … in …** ~가 ~에서 ~를 준비하는 중입니다.
  - He**'s preparing** snacks **in** the kitchen. 그가 부엌에서 스낵을 준비하는 중입니다.
  - Mom **is preparing** dinner **in** the kitchen. 엄마가 부엌에서 저녁을 준비하는 중입니다.

- **Could you help me with …?** ~ 좀 도와줄 수 있어요?
  - **Could you help me with** this banner**?** 배너 거는 것 좀 도와줄 수 있어요?
  - **Could you help me with** this table**?** 이 테이블 좀 도와줄 수 있어요?

■ STUDY TIP

'put up'의 다양한 쓰임:

1. ~을 세우다, 올리다
We put up the ladder against the wall.
우리는 사다리를 벽에 기대 세웠다.

2. (값을) 올리다
They've put up the rent by 100 dollars a month.
그들은 한 달에 100달러 렌트비를 올렸다.

3. 게시하다, 부착하다
John and Julia put up the banner.
John과 Julia는 배너를 부착했다.

대화를 들어보세요. 그런 다음 롤플레잉을 해보세요.

Hi! Did you bring ¹decorations?
안녕! 장식할 거 가지고 왔어?

Yes. I brought some ²balloons and a ³birthday banner.
그래. 풍선과 생일 배너 가져왔어.

Julia shows her bag to Mary.
Julia는 봉투를 Mary에게 보여준다.

When is Kim coming?
Kim은 언제 오니?

She's coming in about 40 minutes.
40분 정도 있으면 올 거야.

They walk to the ⁴dining room.
그들은 주방으로 걸어간다.

He's preparing snacks in the kitchen.
부엌에서 스낵을 준비하고 있어.

Where's John?
John은 어디 있어?

Mary opens the bag of balloons.
Mary는 풍선이 든 봉투를 연다.

What kind of snacks?
무슨 스낵인데?

We've got ⁵mixed nuts, ⁶crackers, and cheese.
여러 가지 견과류와 크래커, 그리고 치즈를 준비했어.

They blow up some balloons.
그들은 풍선을 분다.

Where should we put the balloons?
풍선 어디 놓지?

Julia ⁷ties some ⁸string to a balloon.
Julia는 풍선을 실로 묶는다.

Let's hang them from the ⁹ceiling.
그것들을 천장에 걸자.

Good idea.
좋은 생각이야.

They ¹⁰decorate the dining room with the balloons.
그들은 주방을 풍선으로 장식한다.

Wow! This looks great! Can I help with anything?
와! 멋있어 보이네! 또 도와줄 것 없니?

John puts some snacks on the table.
John은 스낵을 식탁에 놓는다.

Sure.
물론.

Could you help me with this banner?
배너 거는 일 도와줄 수 있어요?

John and Julia put up the banner.
John과 Julia는 배너를 건다.

MATCHING

올바른 영영 뜻을 B열에서 찾아 A열 옆에 쓰세요.

A	B
____ 1. balloon	a. the wall above you in a room 천장
____ 2. ceiling	b. a room that you eat in 식당(방)
____ 3. decorate	c. to make something look nice by adding items 장식하다
____ 4. dining room	d. to join two things together by making a knot (끈 등으로) 묶다
____ 5. tie	e. a rubber bag filled with air 풍선

CONVERSATION

올바른 영어 표현으로 쓰고 말해보세요.

3 _____?
Kim은 언제 오니?

Hi! 1 _____ decorations?
안녕! 장식할 거 가지고 왔어?

Yes. I brought
2 _____.
그래. 풍선과 생일 배너 가져왔어.

She's coming in about 40 minutes.

He's preparing snacks
4 _____.
부엌에서 스낵을 준비하고 있어.

Where's John?

We've got
6 _____.
여러 가지 견과류와 크래커, 그리고 치즈를 준비했어.

5 _____?
무슨 스낵인데?

Where should we put the balloons?

Let's hang them
7 _____.
그것들을 천장에 걸자.

Good idea.

Wow! 8 _____!
Can I help with anything?
와! 멋있어 보이네! 또 도와줄 것 없나요?

Sure.

9 _____?
배너 거는 일 도와줄 수 있어요?

SECTION 9 SPECIAL OCCASIONS 109

SPECIAL OCCASIONS
DAY 44

선물 포장하기
Wrapping a Gift

■ KEY VOCABULARY

wrap	(포장지 등으로) 싸다, 포장하다
wrapping paper	포장지
scissors	가위
tape	테이프
vase	꽃병
unroll (ant. roll)	펼치다, 펴지다
cut off	~을 자르다
cheap (ant. expensive)	(값이) 싼
fold up	반듯하게 접다
tear off	찢어내다
bow	(리본 등의) 나비매듭

■ KEY EXPRESSIONS

- **I got ... (사람) ... (사물)**
  ~을 위해 ~을 준비했어요.
  - **I got** her a vase for flowers.
    그녀를 위해 꽃병을 하나 준비했어요.
  - **I got** my mom some flowers.
    엄마를 위해 꽃을 준비했어요.

- **I got it for ...**   ~에 샀어요.
  - **I got it for** $25.
    25달러에 샀어요.
  - **I got it for** a song.
    엄청 싸게 샀어요.

- **... be on sale.**   ~가 할인 판매하고 있어요.
  - All their vases **are on sale.**
    모든 꽃병을 할인 판매하고 있어요.
  - These flowers **are** all **on sale.**
    이 꽃들을 다 할인 판매하고 있어요.

- **When does ... end?**   ~가 언제 끝나요?
  - **When does** the sale **end?**
    할인 기간은 언제 끝나나요?
  - **When does** the event **end?**
    이 행사는 언제 끝나나요?

■ STUDY TIP

미국에서는 선물을 많이 주고받는다. 크고 비싼 선물보다는 작은 선물과 카드로 서로 마음을 전한다. 미국의 마트에는 카드 코너가 항상 있는데 다양한 종류의 상황에 대한 카드를 많이 판매한다.

대화를 들어보세요. 그런 다음 롤플레잉을 해보세요.

Mary brings out some [2]wrapping paper, [3]scissors, and [4]tape.
Mary는 포장지와 가위 그리고 테이프를 가져온다.

Mary takes a vase out of a shopping bag.
Mary는 쇼핑백에서 꽃병을 꺼낸다.

Mary [6]unrolls some wrapping paper.
Mary는 포장지를 푼다.

She [7]cuts off a sheet of paper.
그녀는 종이 한 장을 잘라낸다.

Mary places the box on the paper and [9]folds up the sides.
Mary는 상자를 포장지에 올려놓고 양쪽 끝을 올려 접는다.

Julia [10]tears off some tape and gives it to Mary.
Julia는 테이프를 잘라 Mary에게 준다.

Mary folds the ends and tapes the paper.
Mary는 끝부분을 접어 포장지에 테이프를 붙인다.

Mary places a [11]bow on the box.
Mary는 상자에 나비매듭을 한다.

MATCHING

올바른 영영 뜻을 B열에서 찾아 A열 옆에 쓰세요.

A	B
____ 1. vase	a. a ribbon you add to a gift (리본 등의) 나비매듭
____ 2. cheap	b. a jar that holds flowers 꽃병
____ 3. scissors	c. a tool used for cutting 가위
____ 4. tear off	d. costing very little money (값이) 싼
____ 5. bow	e. to remove quickly 찢어내다

CONVERSATION

올바른 영어 표현으로 쓰고 말해보세요.

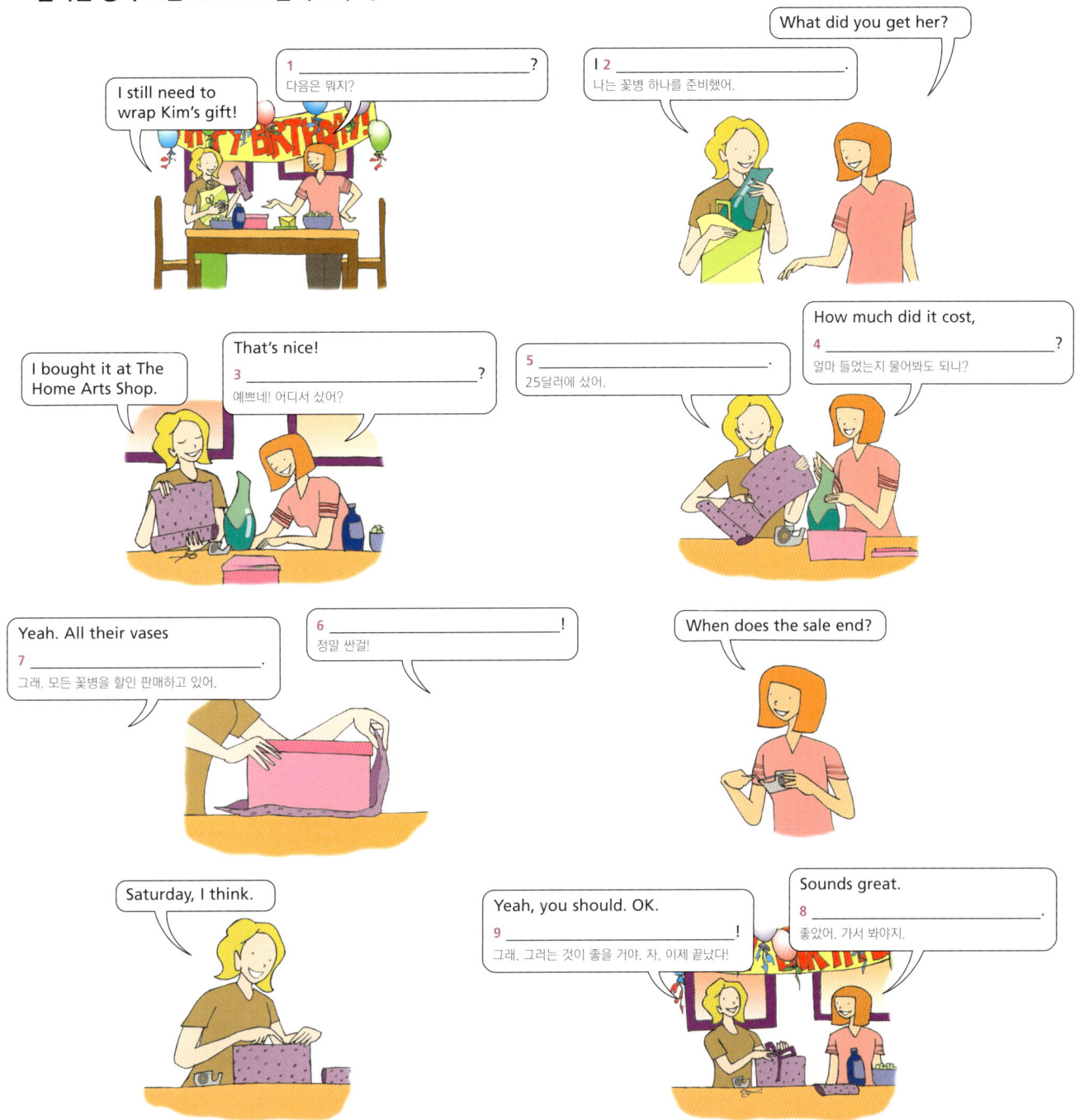

SPECIAL OCCASIONS

DAY 45

파티에서
At the Party

KEY VOCABULARY

arrive	도착하다
present (syn. gift)	선물
light	불을 붙이다
candle	양초
make a wish	소원을 빌다
blow out	(불 등을 불어서) 끄다
unwrap (ant. wrap up)	(포장지 등을) 풀다

KEY EXPRESSIONS

- **Did you make …?** ~을 만들었어요?
  - **Did you make** the cake? 케이크를 만들었어요?
  - **Did you make** the dish? 이 요리를 만들었어요?

- **Don't forget to …** ~하는 거 잊지 마세요.
  - **Don't forget to** make a wish. 소원 비는 거 잊지 마세요.
  - **Don't forget to** give dad your gift. 아빠에게 선물 주는 거 잊지 마세요.

STUDY TIP

와줘서 고마움을 이야기할 때 사용할 수 있는 표현:

Thanks for coming.
Thanks for coming over.
Thank you for coming out.
I'm so glad you made it.

대화를 들어보세요. 그런 다음 롤플레잉을 해보세요.

Peter ¹arrives at the party.
Peter는 파티 장소에 도착한다.

Mary takes the ²present from Peter.
Mary는 Peter에게서 선물을 받아든다.

Peter greets Kim and the others.
Peter는 Kim과 다른 친구들에게 인사한다.

Mary brings in the birthday cake.
Mary는 생일 케이크를 가져온다.

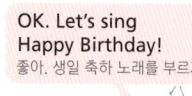

John ³lights the ⁴candles on the cake.
John은 케이크에 있는 양초에 불을 붙인다.

Kim ⁶blows out the candles.
Kim은 촛불을 불어 끈다.

Kim picks up a present.
Kim은 선물을 들어 올린다.

Kim ⁷unwraps the present.
Kim은 선물 포장을 푼다.

MATCHING

올바른 영영 뜻을 B열에서 찾아 A열 옆에 쓰세요.

A		B	
___	1. arrive	a.	to set on fire 불을 붙이다
___	2. candle	b.	to get to a place 도착하다
___	3. light	c.	to open a gift (포장지 등을) 풀다
___	4. present	d.	a stick of wax you set on fire 양초
___	5. unwrap	e.	a gift 선물

CONVERSATION

올바른 영어 표현으로 쓰고 말해보세요.

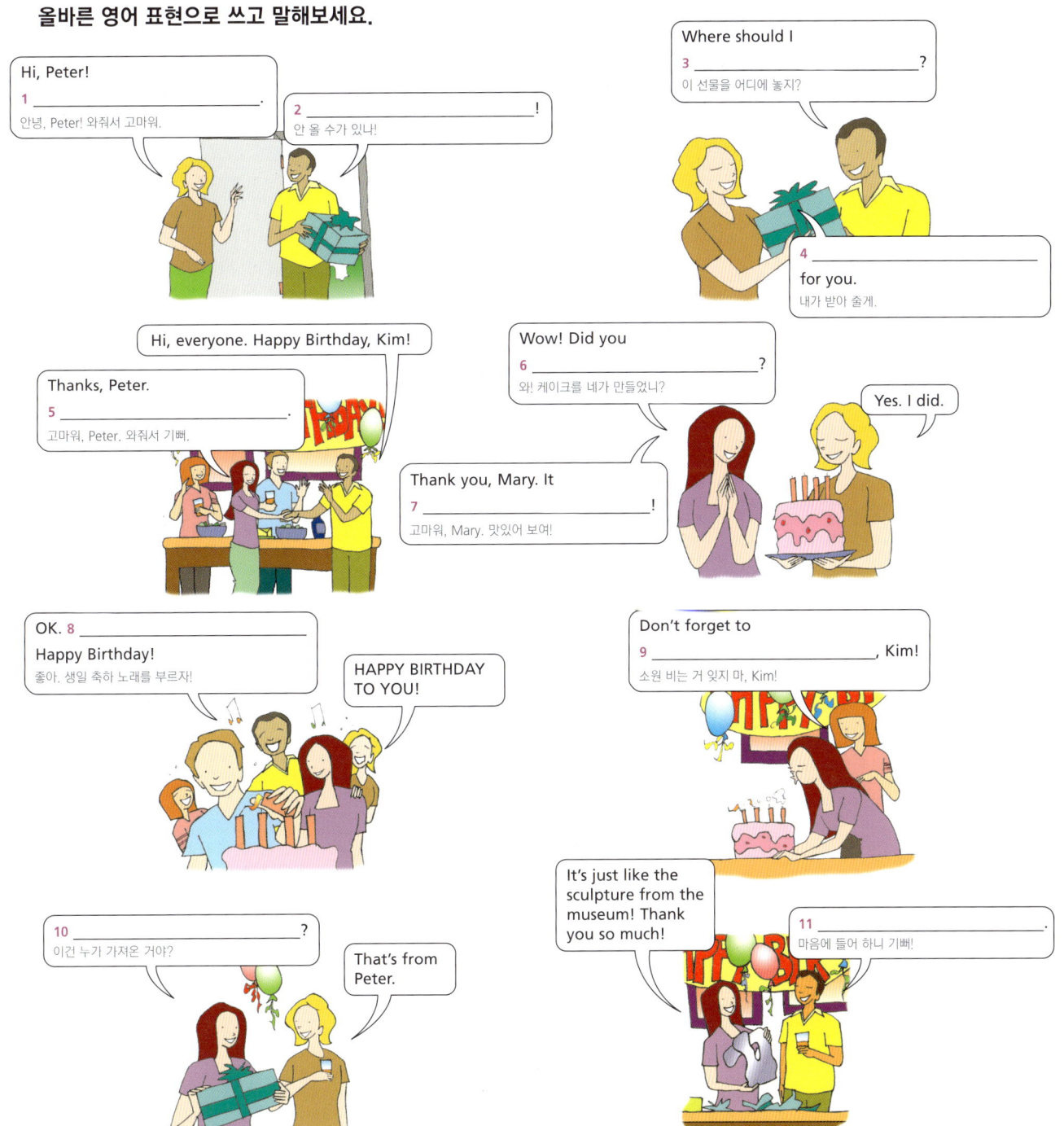

SECTION 10

Descriptions
묘사하기

DAY 46 Getting a Haircut
이발하기

DAY 47 Lost and Found
분실물

DAY 48 A Cooking Lesson
요리 실습

DAY 49 The Date
데이트

DAY 50 A Movie Discussion
영화 얘기

DESCRIPTIONS
DAY 46

이발하기
Getting a Haircut

KEY VOCABULARY

haircut	이발, 머리 깎기
barber	이발사
trim	(끝부분을 잘라내거나 하여) 다듬다
mirror	거울
trimmer	트리머, 다듬는 기계
owe	(돈을) 빚지고 있다
brush off	(먼지 등을) 털다

KEY EXPRESSIONS

- **Just ... (헤어스타일), please.**
  (머리를) 그냥 ~ 해주세요.
  - **Just** trim it**, please.**
    그냥 살짝 다듬어 주세요.
  - **Just** a little off the top**, please.**
    윗부분 조금만 잘라주세요.

- **Do you live in ...?** ~ 에 사시나요?
  - **Do you live in** Austin**?**
    오스틴에 사시나요?
  - **Do you live in** Philadelphia**?**
    필라델피아에 사시나요?

- **Do you want me to ...?** ~ 해드릴까요?
  - **Do you want me to** wash your hair**?**
    머리 감겨드릴까요?
  - **Do you want me to** shampoo your hair**?**
    샴푸 해드릴까요?

STUDY TIP

미용실에서 사용할 수 있는 표현:

Do you take walk-ins?
예약 안 한 손님도 받나요?

Can I get a perm?
파마 가능한가요?

Would you please make me like this picture?
이 사진처럼 제 머리를 해주실래요?

Would you please thin my hair out?
머리숱을 쳐주시겠어요?

I would like bangs.
앞머리를 내고 싶어요.

대화를 들어보세요. 그런 다음 롤플레잉을 해보세요.

John hangs up his jacket.
John은 재킷을 건다.

The [2]barber points to an empty barber chair.
이발사는 비어있는 의자를 가리킨다.

The barber puts an apron on John.
이발사는 덮개를 John에게 씌운다.

The barber cuts John's hair.
이발사는 John의 머리를 깎는다.

John looks in the [4]mirror.
John은 거울을 본다.

The barber trims John's sideburns with a [5]trimmer.
이발사는 John의 구레나룻을 트리머로 다듬는다.

John stands up and [7]brushes himself off.
John은 일어서서 털어낸다.

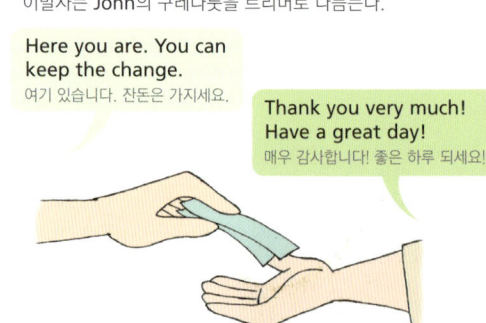

John gives fifteen dollars to the barber.
John은 15달러를 이발사에게 건넨다.

MATCHING

올바른 영영 뜻을 B열에서 찾아 A열 옆에 쓰세요.

A	B
____ 1. barber	a. a piece of glass you can see yourself in 거울
____ 2. haircut	b. the act of cutting your hair 이발
____ 3. mirror	c. to make something a little shorter (끝부분을 잘라내거나 하여) 다듬다
____ 4. owe	d. a person who cuts hair as a job 이발사
____ 5. trim	e. to need to give something to someone (돈을) 빚지고 있다

CONVERSATION

올바른 영어 표현으로 쓰고 말해보세요.

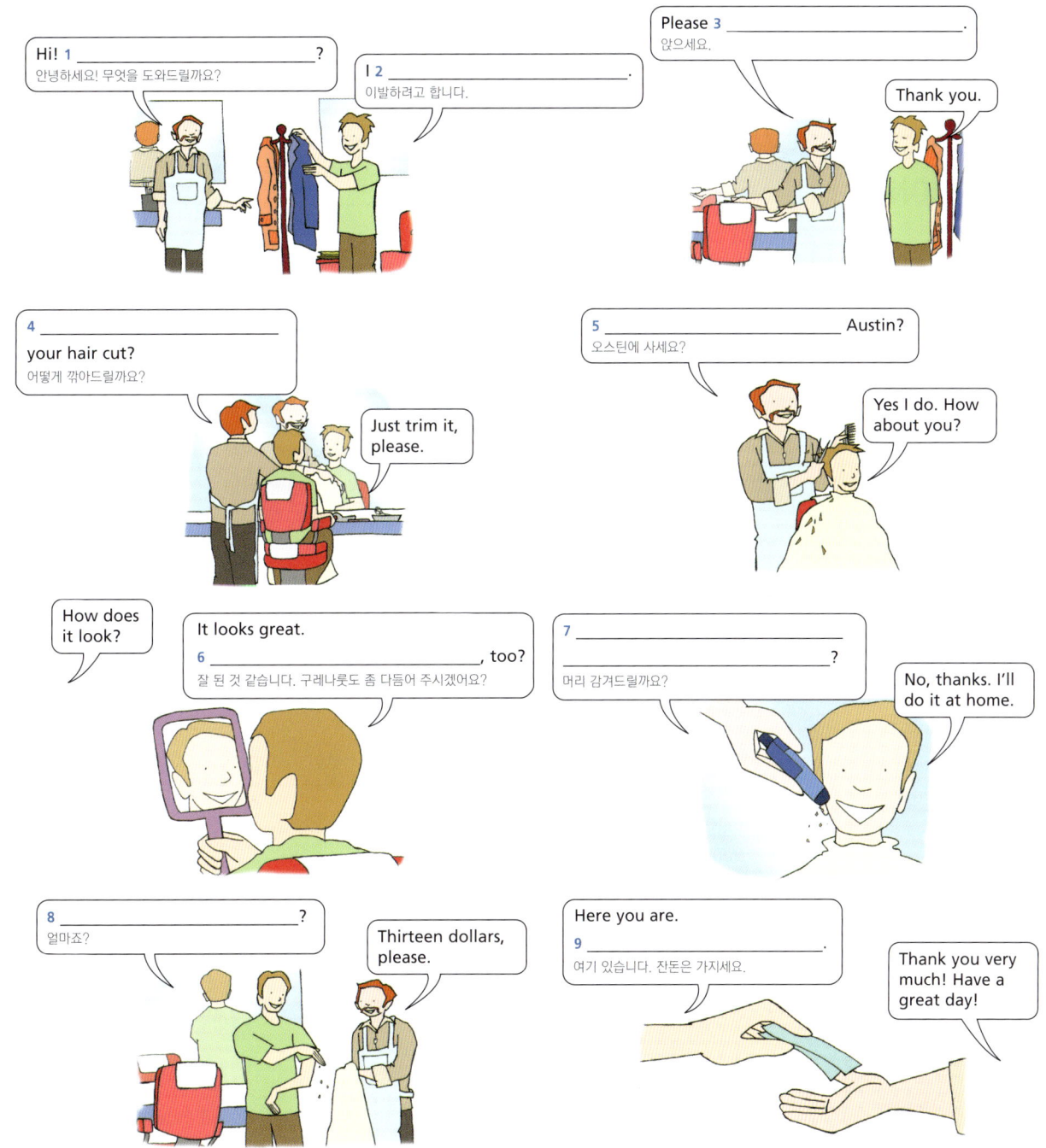

Hi! 1 _____? 안녕하세요! 무엇을 도와드릴까요?

I 2 _____. 이발하려고 합니다.

Please 3 _____. 앉으세요.

Thank you.

4 _____ your hair cut? 어떻게 깎아드릴까요?

Just trim it, please.

5 _____ Austin? 오스틴에 사세요?

Yes I do. How about you?

How does it look?

It looks great. 6 _____, too? 잘 된 것 같습니다. 구레나룻도 좀 다듬어 주시겠어요?

7 _____? 머리 감겨드릴까요?

No, thanks. I'll do it at home.

8 _____? 얼마죠?

Thirteen dollars, please.

Here you are. 9 _____. 여기 있습니다. 잔돈은 가지세요.

Thank you very much! Have a great day!

DESCRIPTIONS
DAY 47
분실물
Lost and Found

─ KEY VOCABULARY

lose	잃어버리다, 분실하다
sports bag	스포츠 가방
brand	상표, 브랜드
detail	세부사항
nylon	나일론
canvas	캔버스 천
strap	끈
running shoes	운동화
sweatshirt	운동복 상의
baseball cap	야구 모자
list	열거하다
content	(어떤 것의) 속에 든 것들, 내용물
contact information	연락처
turn up	(잃어버렸던 물건 등이) 나타나다

─ KEY EXPRESSIONS

- **I think I left …** ~를 놓고 간 것 같아요.
  - **I think I left** my bag here.
    가방을 여기 놓고 간 것 같아요.
  - **I think I left** my wallet there.
    지갑을 거기 놓고 온 것 같아요.

- **What was in …?** ~에 무엇이 들어있나요?
  - **What was in** it?
    무엇이 들어 있었나요?
  - **What was in** the wallet?
    그 지갑에 무엇이 들어 있었나요?

- **It had … in it.** ~이 있었어요.
  - **It had** a pair of running shoes, a sweatshirt, and a baseball cap **in it**.
    운동화 한 켤레와 운동복 상의, 그리고 야구모자가 들어있었어요.
  - **It had** my credit card and my ID **in it**.
    제 신용카드와 신분증이 있었어요.

- **Can I have your …?** 당신의 ~를 주실래요?
  - **Can I have your** name, please?
    이름을 알려주실래요?
  - **Can I have your** phone number, please?
    당신의 연락처를 주실래요?

─ STUDY TIP

다양한 가방 종류:

Tote   Backpack   Satchel Bag

대화를 들어보세요. 그런 다음 롤플레잉을 해보세요.

Excuse me. **I think I left** my bag here. Has anybody found one?
실례합니다, 가방을 여기 놓고 간 것 같은데요. 누가 본 사람 없나요?

Peter tells the employee that he ¹lost his bag.
Peter는 종업원에게 가방을 잃어버렸다고 말한다.

No, I'm afraid not. What kind of bag is it?
없는 것 같은데요. 어떤 가방이죠?

It's a green ²sports bag.
초록색 스포츠 가방이에요.

Peter describes his bag.
Peter는 가방이 어떻게 생겼는지 설명한다.

What ³brand is it?
상표는 뭐죠?

Pro-Sports.
프로스포츠에요.

The woman writes down the ⁴details.
여종업원은 세부 내용을 적어 놓는다.

How big is it?
얼마나 크죠?

About this big.
이 정도쯤 돼요.

Peter shows the size of the bag with his hands.
Peter는 손으로 가방의 크기를 보여준다.

What is it made of?
소재는 뭐죠?

It's ⁵nylon with ⁶canvas ⁷straps.
캔버스 천의 끈이 달린 나일론 가방이에요.

Peter describes the material.
Peter는 소재를 설명한다.

What was in it?
무엇이 들어있나요?

It had a pair of ⁸running shoes, a ⁹sweatshirt, and a ¹⁰baseball cap in it.
운동화 한 켤레와 운동복 상의, 그리고 야구모자가 들어있었어요.

Peter ¹¹lists the ¹²contents of the bag.
Peter는 가방의 내용물을 열거한다.

Can I have your name, please?
성함이 어떻게 되시죠?

Sure. It's Peter Waynans. And my phone number is 239-8985.
Peter Waynans고, 연락처는 239-8985입니다.

Peter leaves his ¹³contact information.
Peter는 자신의 연락처를 남긴다.

OK, Mr. Waynans. We'll contact you if it ¹⁴turns up.
알았습니다, Waynans씨. 찾으면 연락드릴게요.

Thank you very much.
고맙습니다.

She offers to call Peter if the bag is found.
그녀는 가방을 찾게 되면 Peter에게 연락하겠다고 한다.

SECTION 10 DESCRIPTIONS

MATCHING

올바른 영영 뜻을 B열에서 찾아 A열 옆에 쓰세요.

A	B
____ 1. baseball cap	a. shoes you wear while exercising 운동화
____ 2. contact information	b. to write names or items on a piece of paper 열거하다
____ 3. lose	c. a hat that a baseball player wears 야구 모자
____ 4. list	d. your name, phone number, and email address 연락처
____ 5. running shoes	e. to no longer have 잃어버리다

CONVERSATION

올바른 영어 표현으로 쓰고 말해보세요.

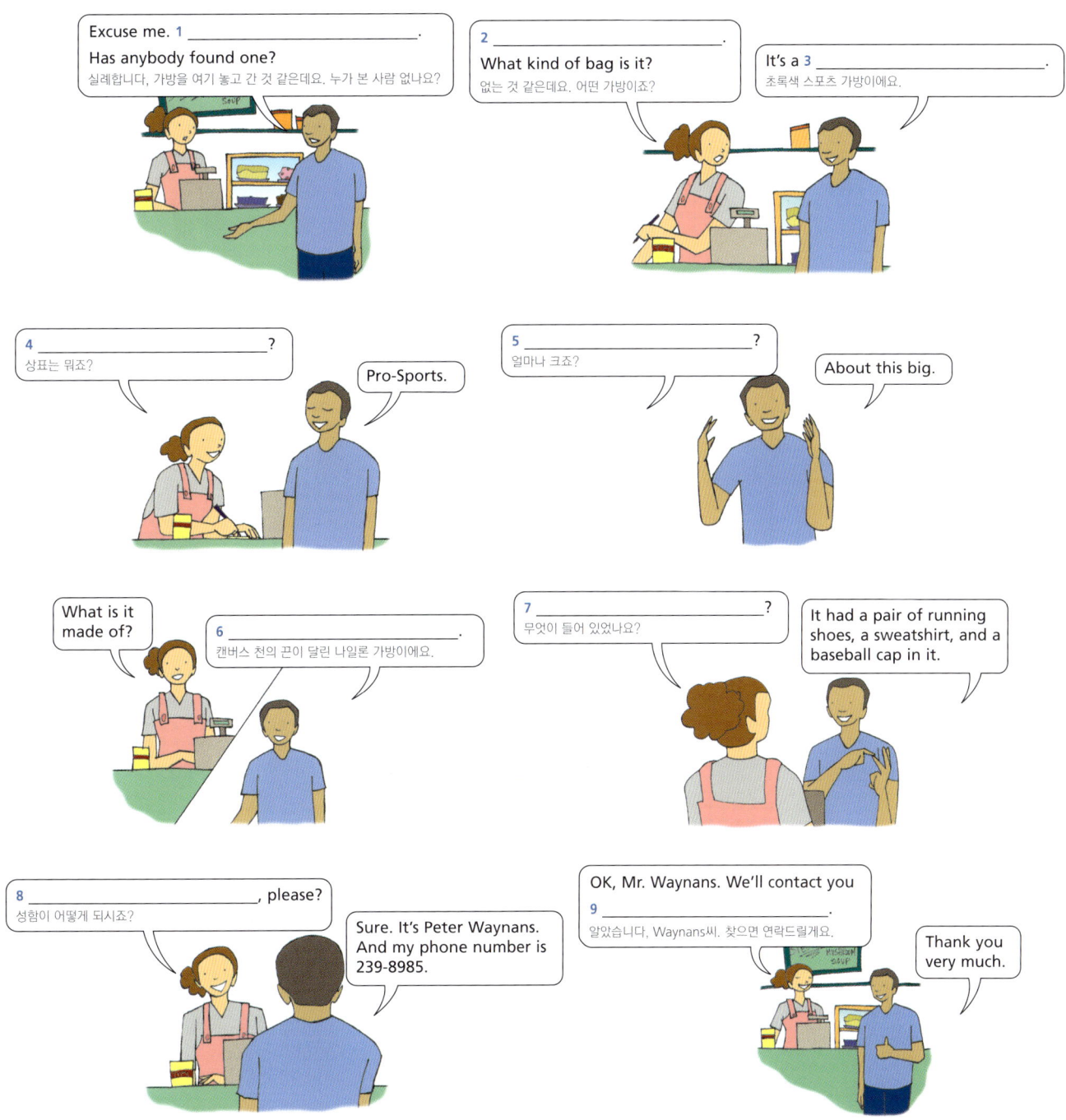

DESCRIPTIONS
DAY 48
요리 실습
A Cooking Lesson

KEY VOCABULARY

recipe	조리법, 요리법
wash hands	손을 씻다
grate	갈다
vegetable	채소, 야채
chop up	작게 썰다
onion	양파
pepper	고추
fry	튀기다, 볶다
butter	버터
frying pan	프라이팬
stove	스토브
chicken breast	닭가슴살
oven	오븐
slice	(얇게) 썰다, 저미다
sprinkle	뿌리다

KEY EXPRESSIONS

- **What are we ...ing?**
  우리는 ~ 을 하나요?
  - **What are we** mak**ing?**
    우리 뭐 만들어?
  - **What are we** bak**ing?**
    우리는 무엇을 굽나요?

- **How much ... do we need?**
  얼마만큼의 ~ 가 필요한가요?
  - **How much** cheese **do we need?**
    얼마만큼의 치즈가 필요한가요?
  - **How much** sugar **do we need?**
    얼마만큼의 설탕이 필요한가요?

- **They look ...** ~ 해 보이네요.
  - **They look** perfect!
    완벽해 보이네요!
  - **They look** burnt!
    타 보이네요.

- **... take ... out of ...**
  ~ 가 ~ 를 ~ 에서 꺼내다
  - Julia **takes** a pan of chicken breasts **out of** the oven.
    Julia는 닭가슴살 요리를 오븐에서 꺼낸다.
  - Mark **takes** the chicken **out of** the refrigerator.
    Mark는 닭을 냉장고에서 꺼낸다.

STUDY TIP

파히타(fajita)는 토르티야에 다양한 야채와 고기 등을 싸 먹는 멕시코 요리의 하나이다. 양파와 파프리카를 같이 넣어 볶는 게 일반적이며, 사워크림, 살사, 치즈, 토마토소스 등을 곁들여 먹는다.

대화를 들어보세요. 그런 다음 롤플레잉을 해보세요.

What are we making?
우리 뭐 만들어?

Chicken fajitas. It's my grandmother's ¹recipe.
닭고기 파히타. 우리 할머니의 요리법이야.

faucet 수도꼭지

Kim ²washes her hands in the kitchen sink.
Kim은 부엌 싱크대에서 손을 씻는다.

Sounds delicious! What should I do?
맛있을 것 같네! 나는 뭘 해야지?

First, ³grate this cheese.
먼저, 이 치즈를 갈아줘.

grater 강판

Julia hands Kim a piece of cheese and a grater.
Julia는 Kim에게 치즈와 강판을 준다.

How much cheese do we need?
치즈는 얼마나 필요하니?

About half a cup.
반 컵 정도.

Kim grates the cheese while Julia washes the ⁴vegetables.
Julia가 채소를 씻는 동안 Kim이 치즈를 간다.

What's next?
다음은?

Please ⁵chop up these ⁶onions and ⁷peppers.
이 양파와 고추를 잘게 썰어줘.

Julia puts the vegetables on a cutting board.
Julia는 채소를 도마에 올려놓는다.

Great! Now ⁸fry them in ⁹butter for about five minutes.
좋아! 이제 버터를 넣고 5분 정도 볶을 거야.

Is this OK?
됐냐?

cutting board 도마

Julia puts a ¹⁰frying pan on the ¹¹stove.
Julia는 프라이팬을 스토브에 올려놓는다.

Do you think these are done?
이제 되었을까?

Yes. They look perfect!
그래. 완벽해 보이네.

Julia **takes** a pan of ¹²chicken breasts **out of** the ¹³oven.
Julia는 닭가슴살 요리를 오븐에서 꺼낸다.

Mmmm. That smells great! Anything else?
음. 냄새 좋은데! 할 게 또 있니?

No. After I cut up this chicken we can eat!
아니. 이제 닭고기를 자르기만 하면 먹을 수 있어!

Julia ¹⁴slices the chicken breasts into strips.
Julia는 닭가슴살을 길고 얇게 자른다.

Wow! This looks fantastic!
와! 정말 훌륭해 보이네!

We have plenty, so please help yourself to more.
충분히 만들었으니, 더 먹어.

Kim ¹⁵sprinkles some cheese on her fajita.
Kim은 치즈를 화이타에 뿌린다.

MATCHING

올바른 영영 뜻을 B열에서 찾아 A열 옆에 쓰세요.

A	B
____ 1. butter	a. to cook in oil or butter 튀기다, 볶다
____ 2. fry	b. a set of directions for making a food 조리법
____ 3. onion	c. a vegetable with many white layers 양파
____ 4. recipe	d. a yellow solid food containing a lot of fat 버터
____ 5. slice	e. to cut something into thin pieces (얇게) 썰다

CONVERSATION

올바른 영어 표현으로 쓰고 말해보세요.

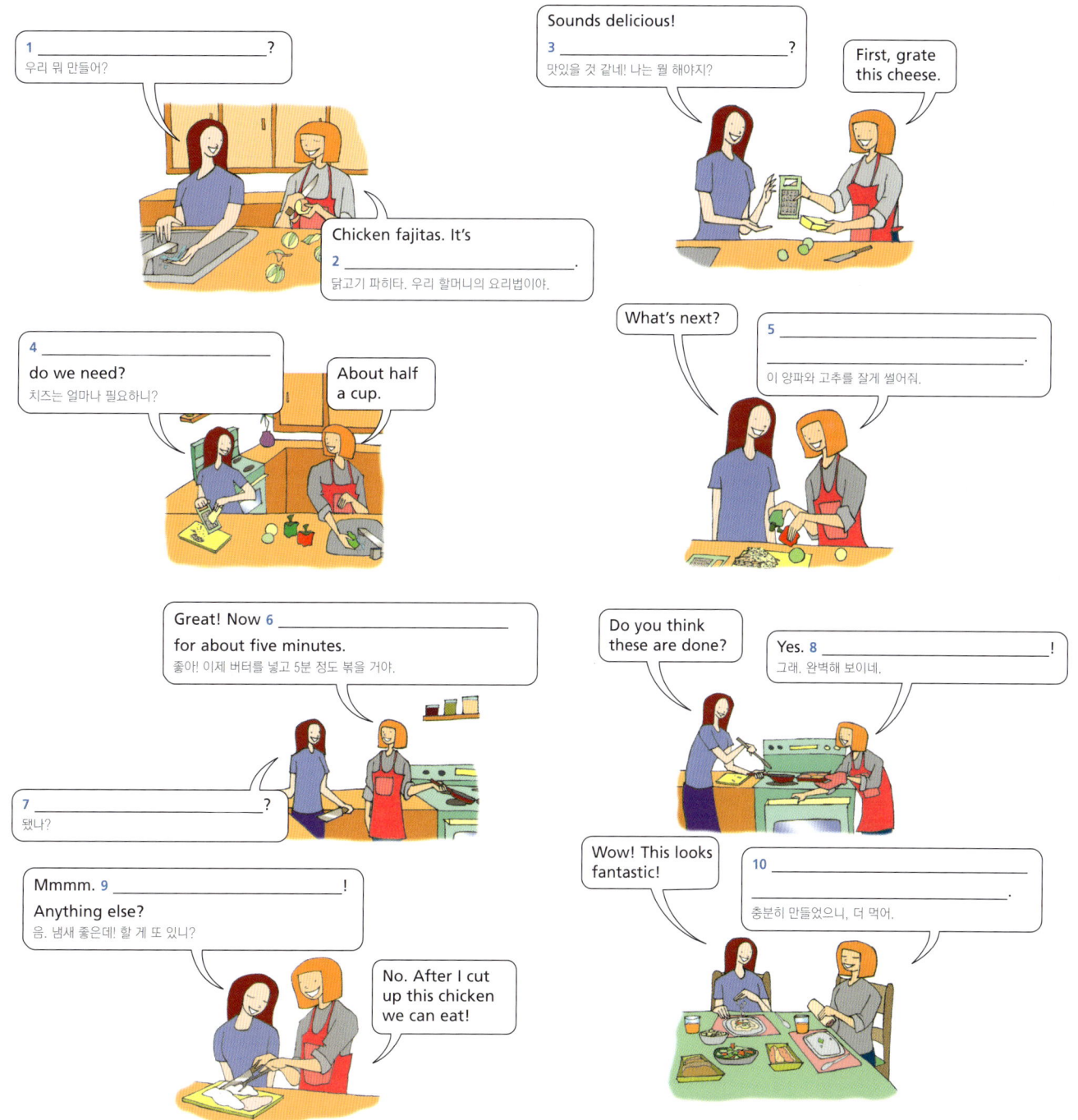

1 _____?
우리 뭐 만들어?

Chicken fajitas. It's 2 _____.
닭고기 파히타. 우리 할머니의 요리법이야.

Sounds delicious! 3 _____?
맛있을 것 같네! 나는 뭘 해야지?

First, grate this cheese.

4 _____ do we need?
치즈는 얼마나 필요하니?

About half a cup.

What's next?

5 _____.
이 양파와 고추를 잘게 썰어줘.

Great! Now 6 _____ for about five minutes.
좋아! 이제 버터를 넣고 5분 정도 볶을 거야.

Do you think these are done?

Yes. 8 _____!
그래. 완벽해 보이네.

7 _____?
됐나?

Mmmm. 9 _____! Anything else?
음. 냄새 좋은데! 할 게 또 있니?

Wow! This looks fantastic!

10 _____.
충분히 만들었으니, 더 먹어.

No. After I cut up this chicken we can eat!

SECTION 10 DESCRIPTIONS 121

DESCRIPTIONS
DAY 49
데이트
The Date

KEY VOCABULARY

weekend	주말 (토요일과 일요일)
scrape	(떼어 내기 위해) 긁다, 긁어내다
fill	채우다
soap	비누
river	강
rubber gloves	고무장갑
handsome (syn. good-looking)	멋진, 잘생긴
rinse	씻다, 씻어 내다
sense of humor	유머 감각
hit it off	죽이 맞다, 잘 통하다
dry off	~을 말리다
dishtowel	마른행주

KEY EXPRESSIONS

- **What did you do …?** ~에 뭐 했나요?
  - **What did you do** last **weekend**?
    지난 주말에 뭐 했나요?
  - **What did you** do last month?
    지난달에 뭐 했나요?

- **We went to …** ~에 갔어요.
  - **We went to** the Italian restaurant by the river.
    강가에 있는 이탈리아 식당에 갔어요.
  - **We went to** a popular taco restaurant downtown.
    시내에 있는 유명한 타코 식당에 갔어요.

- **What does … look like?**
  ~는 어떻게 생겼어요?
  - **What does** he **look like?**
    그는 어떻게 생겼어요?
  - **What does** she **look like?**
    그녀는 어떻게 생겼어요?

- **… has …** (생김새 표현)
  ~는 ~ 생겼어요.
  - He **has** dark hair and a great smile.
    그는 검은 머리에 웃는 모습이 멋있어요.
  - He **has** dark hair and dark eyes.
    그는 까만 머리에 까만 눈을 가졌어요.

STUDY TIP

'hit it off'는 '잘 통하다, 죽이 맞다, 코드가 맞다.' 라는 표현으로 오랜 관계에서보다는 주로 첫 만남에서 쓰이는 표현이다.

We really hit it off.
우리 잘 통하네.

I didn't hit it off with my boyfriend at first.
처음에는 남자친구와 잘 안 맞았어요.

대화를 들어보세요. 그런 다음 롤플레잉을 해보세요.

What did you do last ¹weekend?
지난주에 뭐 했어?

I had a date with a guy named Mark.
Mark라는 남자와 데이트 했어.

Kim ²scrapes the plates into the garbage can.
Kim은 접시에 있는 것을 쓰레기통으로 쓸어 넣는다.

How did it go?
어땠니?

I had a great time!
좋은 시간 보냈어!

They ³fill the sink with hot water.
그들은 개수대를 따뜻한 물로 채운다.

What did you do?
뭐 했는데?

He took me out to dinner.
그가 나를 데리고 나가서 저녁 식사를 했어.

Julia puts in some ⁴soap.
Julia는 비누를 넣는다.

Where did you go?
어디 갔는데?

We went to the Italian restaurant by the ⁵river.
강가에 있는 이탈리아 식당에 갔어.

She puts on some ⁶rubber gloves…
그녀는 고무장갑을 낀다.

How was it?
어땠어?

Great! The food was wonderful and the restaurant was very romantic.
좋았지! 음식도 좋고 분위기도 매우 낭만적이었어.

…and washes a plate.
그리고 접시를 씻는다.

So, tell me about Mark. What does he look like?
그럼, Mark에 대해 얘기해 봐. 어떻게 생겼어?

He's very ⁷handsome. He has dark hair and a great smile.
무척 잘 생겼어. 검은 머리에, 웃는 모습이 정말 멋져.

Kim takes the plate and ⁸rinses it.
Kim은 접시를 헹군다.

What is he like?
사람은 어때?

He is so nice! And he has a great ⁹sense of humor.
굉장히 좋아! 게다가 유머 감각도 뛰어나고.

dish rack
그릇 선반

Kim puts the plate into the dish rack.
Kim은 접시를 그릇 선반에 넣는다.

Sounds like you guys really ¹⁰hit it off!
잘 통하는 것 같네!

Yeah. We're going out again this weekend.
그래. 우리 이번 주말에 다시 데이트하기로 했어.

Kim ¹¹dries off a glass with a ¹²dishtowel.
Kim은 마른행주로 컵의 물기를 닦아낸다.

MATCHING

올바른 영영 뜻을 B열에서 찾아 A열 옆에 쓰세요.

A	B
____ 1. dishtowel	a. good-looking 멋진
____ 2. handsome	b. a piece of cloth you dry the dishes with 마른행주
____ 3. hit it off	c. to wash something with water 씻다
____ 4. rinse	d. to become friends quickly 잘 통하다
____ 5. weekend	e. Saturday and Sunday 주말 (토요일과 일요일)

CONVERSATION

올바른 영어 표현으로 쓰고 말해보세요.

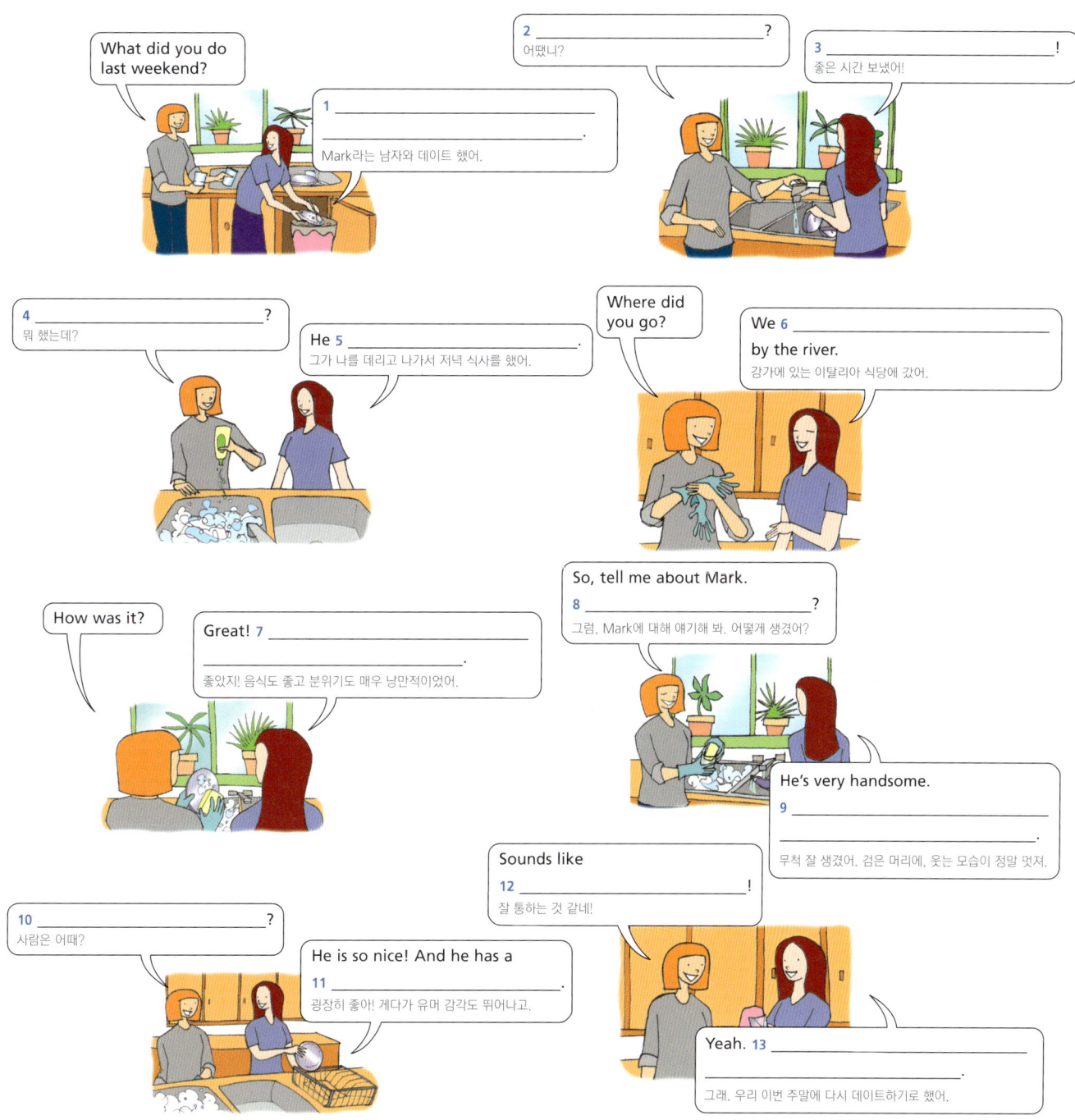

What did you do last weekend?

1 _____.
Mark라는 남자와 데이트 했어.

2 _____?
어땠니?

3 _____!
좋은 시간 보냈어!

4 _____?
뭐 했는데?

He 5 _____.
그가 나를 데리고 나가서 저녁 식사를 했어.

Where did you go?

We 6 _____ by the river.
강가에 있는 이탈리아 식당에 갔어.

How was it?

Great! 7 _____.
좋았지! 음식도 좋고 분위기도 매우 낭만적이었어.

So, tell me about Mark.
8 _____?
그럼, Mark에 대해 얘기해 봐. 어떻게 생겼어?

He's very handsome.
9 _____.
무척 잘 생겼어. 검은 머리에, 옷는 모습이 정말 멋져.

10 _____?
사람은 어때?

He is so nice! And he has a
11 _____.
굉장히 좋아! 게다가 유머 감각도 뛰어나고.

Sounds like
12 _____!
잘 통하는 것 같네!

Yeah. 13 _____.
그래. 우리 이번 주말에 다시 데이트하기로 했어.

SECTION 10 DESCRIPTIONS 123

DESCRIPTIONS
DAY 50
영화 얘기
A Movie Discussion

■ KEY VOCABULARY

subway	지하철
romantic movie	로맨틱 영화
sci-fi	공상 과학의
platform	(기차역의) 플랫폼
special effect	특수 효과
passenger	승객
actor	배우
role	(배우의) 역할, 배역

■ KEY EXPRESSIONS

- **What are you doing …?**
  ~ 에 뭐 할 생각이에요?
  - **What are you doing** this weekend**?**
    이번 주말에 뭐 할 생각이에요?
  - **What are you doing** tomorrow night**?**
    내일 저녁에 뭐 할 생각이에요?

- **… be going to …** ~ 하려고요.
  - Mary and I **are going to** see a movie.
    Mary와 저는 영화 보러 가려고요.
  - Sam and I **are going to** see a play.
    Sam과 저는 연극을 보러 가려고요.

- **How did you like …?** ~ 는 어땠어요?
  - **How did you like** the special effects?
    특수효과는 어땠어요?
  - **How did you like** the special cast?
    특별 출연진은 어땠어요?

- **I like … the best.**
  저는 ~ 를 가장 좋아해요.
  - **I like** Al Pacino **the best.**
    저는 Al Pacino를 가장 좋아해요.
  - **I like** Leonardo DiCaprio **the best.**
    저는 Leonardo DiCaprio를 가장 좋아해요.

■ STUDY TIP

다양한 영화 장르:

action movie 액션 영화
documentary movie 다큐멘터리 영화
horror movie 공포 영화
independent movie 독립 영화
martial arts movie 무협 영화

대화를 들어보세요. 그런 다음 롤플레잉을 해보세요.

John and Carlos walk down into the ¹subway.
John과 Carlos는 지하철로 내려간다.

John buys two tickets.
John은 표 2장을 산다.

Carlos touches his ticket to the sensor.
Carlos는 표를 센서에 댄다.

They walk through the turnstiles.
그늘은 회전식 개찰구를 통해 들어간다.

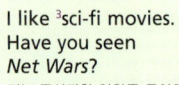

John and Carlos wait on the ⁴platform.
John과 Carlos는 승강장에서 기다린다.

They wait for the other ⁶passengers to get off.
그들은 다른 승객들이 내리도록 기다린다.

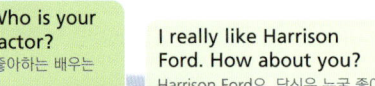

They step onto the train.
그들은 열차에 올라탄다.

They hold on as the subway begins to move.
그들은 지하철이 움직이기 시작하자 손잡이를 잡는다.

MATCHING

올바른 영영 뜻을 B열에서 찾아 A열 옆에 쓰세요.

A
1. actor
2. passenger
3. role
4. romantic movie
5. subway

B
a. a train that goes under the city 지하철
b. someone who is traveling in a car, boat, or airplane but not driving 승객
c. an actor's part in a movie or play (배우의) 역할
d. a movie about love 로맨틱 영화
e. someone who acts in movies or plays 배우

CONVERSATION

올바른 영어 표현으로 쓰고 말해보세요.

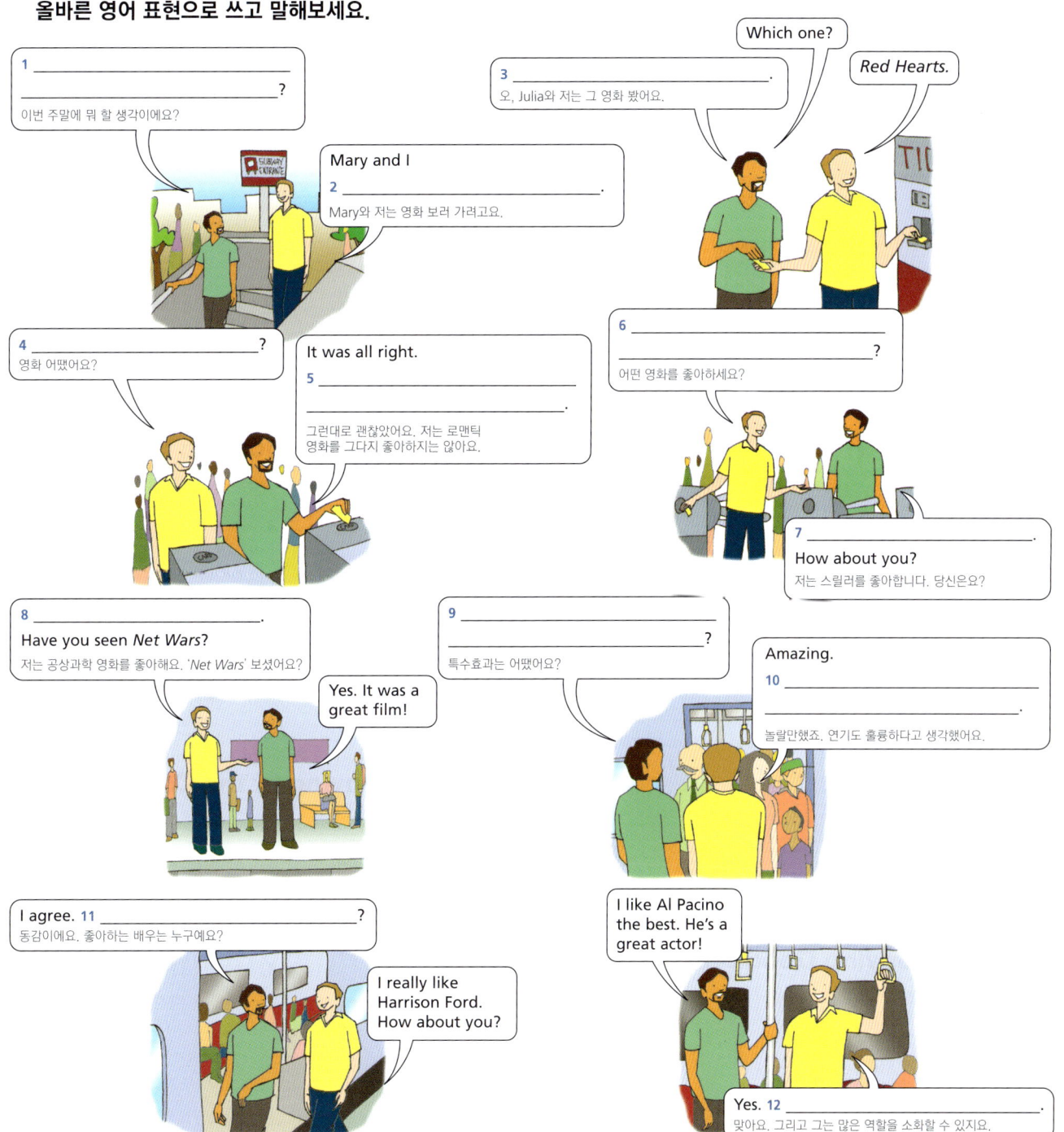

1. _____ ?
이번 주말에 뭐 할 생각이에요?

Mary and I
2. _____.
Mary와 저는 영화 보러 가려고요.

3. _____.
오, Julia와 저는 그 영화 봤어요.

Which one?

Red Hearts.

4. _____ ?
영화 어땠어요?

It was all right.
5. _____
_____.
그런대로 괜찮았어요. 저는 로맨틱 영화를 그다지 좋아하지는 않아요.

6. _____ ?
어떤 영화를 좋아하세요?

7. _____.
How about you?
저는 스릴러를 좋아합니다. 당신은요?

8. _____.
Have you seen Net Wars?
저는 공상과학 영화를 좋아해요. 'Net Wars' 보셨어요?

Yes. It was a great film!

9. _____ ?
특수효과는 어땠어요?

Amazing.
10. _____
_____.
놀랄만했죠. 연기도 훌륭하다고 생각했어요.

I agree. 11. _____ ?
동감이에요. 좋아하는 배우는 누구예요?

I really like Harrison Ford. How about you?

I like Al Pacino the best. He's a great actor!

Yes. 12. _____.
맞아요. 그리고 그는 많은 역할을 소화할 수 있지요.

ANSWER KEY

DAY 1 Introductions

MATCHING

1. c   2. e   3. a   4. b   5. d

CONVERSATION

1. meet
2. call
3. Chicago
4. hometown
5. plans
6. husband

DAY 2 The Visit

MATCHING

1. e   2. a   3. d   4. c   5. b

CONVERSATION

1. Thanks
2. come
3. take
4. neighbor
5. Good
6. go
7. lovely
8. drink
9. have

DAY 3 Occupations

MATCHING

1. a   2. b   3. e   4. c   5. d

CONVERSATION

1. sit
2. How
3. nice
4. company
5. job
6. engineer
7. interesting
8. work
9. bank
10. part-time

DAY 4 School

MATCHING

1. b   2. e   3. c   4. a   5. d

CONVERSATION

1. studying
2. Business
3. major
4. math
5. school
6. sophomore
7. May

DAY 5 Saying Goodbye

MATCHING

1. d   2. b   3. a   4. c   5. e

CONVERSATION

1. get
2. soon
3. bed
4. night owls
5. jar
6. visit
7. night

DAY 6 Women's Clothing

MATCHING

1. c   2. b   3. d   4. e   5. a

CONVERSATION

1. spring clothes
2. good
3. color
4. looking for
5. light blue
6. about
7. medium
8. try

DAY 7 Sizes and Trying Things On

MATCHING

1. b   2. e   3. d   4. c   5. a

CONVERSATION

1. try
2. fit
3. sandals
4. popular
5. size
6. tight
7. better

DAY 8 Men's Clothing

MATCHING

1. e   2. b   3. d   4. a   5. c

CONVERSATION

1. need
2. looking
3. size
4. waist
5. fit
6. sale
7. cotton
8. nice
9. get

DAY 9 Paying at the Counter

MATCHING

1. d   2. e   3. a   4. b   5. c

CONVERSATION

1. try on
2. cash
3. total
4. use
5. receipt
6. exchange
7. come

DAY 10 Electronics

MATCHING

1. b 2. c 3. d 4. e 5. a

CONVERSATION

1. sell
2. easy
3. expensive
4. Germany
5. warranty
6. comes
7. help

DAY 11 At a Fast Food Restaurant

MATCHING

1. c 2. d 3. a 4. e 5. b

CONVERSATION

1. order
2. favorite
3. chocolate
4. pickles
5. here
6. meal
7. ketchup
8. straws
9. delicious

DAY 12 At the Movies

MATCHING

1. e 2. a 3. c 4. b 5. d

CONVERSATION

1. movie
2. tickets
3. popcorn
4. medium
5. Here
6. Screen
7. seats

DAY 13 Helping a Neighbor

MATCHING

1. d 2. c 3. b 4. a 5. e

CONVERSATION

1. help
2. food
3. grandchildren
4. door
5. kitchen
6. fine
7. trash
8. neighbor

DAY 14 At a Coffee Shop

MATCHING

1. c 2. a 3. d 4. e 5. b

CONVERSATION

1. coffee
2. decaf
3. cappuccino
4. drinks
5. low-fat
6. cream
7. museum
8. weekend
9. call

DAY 15 At the Museum

MATCHING

1. e 2. a 3. b 4. d 5. c

CONVERSATION

1. taxi
2. trouble
3. fair
4. guided
5. amazing
6. pictures
7. made
8. favorite

DAY 16 Taking a Taxi

MATCHING

1. b 2. d 3. e 4. a 5. c

CONVERSATION

1. want to
2. take a cab
3. going to
4. not heavy
5. we are
6. the change
7. a nice day

DAY 17 In the Library

MATCHING

1. e 2. a 3. b 4. d 5. c

CONVERSATION

1. kind
2. looking for
3. favorite author
4. famous thief
5. interesting
6. another copy
7. two weeks

DAY 18 Taking a Bus

MATCHING

1. b 2. a 3. d 4. e 5. c

CONVERSATION

1. take bus
2. How often
3. your help
4. How many stops
5. have my seat
6. kind

DAY 19 Getting Gas

MATCHING

1. a 2. d 3. c 4. e 5. b

CONVERSATION
1. gas station
2. get some gas
3. saves money
4. open the cover
5. kind of gas
6. worth
7. bathroom
8. All done

DAY 20 Asking for Directions
MATCHING
1. c 2. e 3. a 4. d 5. b
CONVERSATION
1. ask for directions
2. How can we
3. no idea
4. Pardon me
5. down this road
6. on your right
7. four blocks
8. Have fun

DAY 21 Arriving at the Restaurant
MATCHING
1. c 2. a 3. e 4. d 5. b
CONVERSATION
1. have a reservation
2. have your reservation
3. follow me
4. all right
5. next to
6. Today's special
7. with you

DAY 22 Ordering Drinks and an Appetizer
MATCHING
1. b 2. e 3. d 4. c 5. a
CONVERSATION
1. delicious
2. this evening
3. anything to drink
4. I'd like
5. grape juice
6. Let's get
7. be right back

DAY 23 The Waiter Returns
MATCHING
1. a 2. d 3. b 4. c 5. e
CONVERSATION
1. to order
2. have
3. How would you
4. comes with
5. seafood spaghetti
6. onion soup
7. call me

DAY 24 The Food Arrives
MATCHING
1. b 2. c 3. e 4. a 5. d
CONVERSATION
1. seafood spaghetti
2. all right
3. on your pasta
4. these plates
5. anything else
6. Enjoy

DAY 25 A Lovely Meal
MATCHING
1. b 2. d 3. a 4. e 5. c
CONVERSATION
1. Would you like
2. full
3. Could we have
4. take the rest
5. take your plates
6. excellent dinner

DAY 26 Check-in
MATCHING
1. b 2. e 3. c 4. d 5. a
CONVERSATION
1. passport and ticket
2. mileage card
3. luggage
4. on the scale
5. Did you pack
6. left your suitcase
7. write your name
8. a window seat
9. boarding time

DAY 27 Security
MATCHING
1. c 2. a 3. d 4. b 5. e
CONVERSATION
1. my camera
2. will be fine
3. empty
4. step this way
5. look through
6. for headaches
7. go to immigration
8. nice flight

DAY 28 Boarding
MATCHING
1. d 2. c 3. a 4. e 5. b
CONVERSATION
1. ready for boarding
2. rows 20-40
3. seat 36J
4. go straight
5. put up your bag
6. get by
7. make sure

DAY 29 The Flight

MATCHING
1. a   2. b   3. d   4. e   5. c

CONVERSATION
1. first time
2. on business
3. going on vacation
4. visit my parents
5. chicken or seafood
6. return to your seats
7. seat up
8. Thank you

DAY 30 Immigration (Arrival)

MATCHING
1. c   2. a   3. e   4. d   5. b

CONVERSATION
1. arrival card
2. New York
3. How long
4. for 10 days
5. purpose
6. on vacation
7. staying at
8. baggage claim

DAY 31 Car Rental

MATCHING
1. b   2. c   3. e   4. d   5. a

CONVERSATION
1. rent a car
2. sedans, and SUVs
3. compact car
4. Sounds great
5. fill out
6. insurance
7. free map
8. nice trip

DAY 32 Hotel Check-in

MATCHING
1. e   2. d   3. a   4. b   5. c

CONVERSATION
1. Welcome to
2. How may I
3. check in
4. reservation
5. single room
6. pay for
7. credit card
8. non-smoking room

DAY 33 The Hotel Concierge

MATCHING
1. a   2. e   3. c   4. d   5. b

CONVERSATION
1. would like to visit
2. brochure and map
3. going sightseeing
4. Why don't we
5. How long
6. about an hour
7. opens at
8. Enjoy

DAY 34 Sightseeing

MATCHING
1. c   2. d   3. a   4. b   5. e

CONVERSATION
1. amazing
2. get someone
3. take our picture
4. press
5. in the background
6. move a bit
7. You're welcome

DAY 35 Hotel Check-out

MATCHING
1. d   2. a   3. e   4. b   5. c

CONVERSATION
1. check out
2. your room number
3. Did you use
4. sign it
5. called the airport
6. staying with us

DAY 36 Exercise

MATCHING
1. e   2. b   3. a   4. d   5. c

CONVERSATION
1. get together
2. How often
3. three times a week
4. go to a gym
5. do you like
6. That's why
7. How long

DAY 37 An Accident

MATCHING
1. d   2. a   3. e   4. b   5. c

CONVERSATION
1. Are you
2. sprained my wrist
3. move it
4. it hurts
5. it's broken
6. go home
7. have the keys

DAY 38 In the Doctor's Office

MATCHING
1. e   2. a   3. c   4. b   5. d

CONVERSATION
1. have an appointment
2. insurance card
3. have a seat
4. really bad cold
5. fell down
6. feel better
7. sit here

DAY 39 The Examination

MATCHING

1. d   2. e   3. a   4. b   5. c

CONVERSATION

1. what's the trouble
2. I have a very bad cold
3. Please open your mouth
4. breathe deeply
5. need to take some medicine
6. plenty of fluids

DAY 40 At the Pharmacy

MATCHING

1. d   2. a   3. c   4. b   5. e

CONVERSATION

1. May I help you   2. I'd like to get
3. have a seat   4. medicine is ready
5. How often   6. times a day
7. Can I take it with food   8. don't drink any milk
9. side effects   10. or an upset stomach
11. sore throat   12. soothe the pain

DAY 41 Planning a Party

MATCHING

1. a   2. c   3. b   4. e   5. d

CONVERSATION

1. really like Dr. Haddock
2. do you have plans
3. have a party for her
4. What time
5. That's fine
6. I'm not sure
7. chicken tortillas
8. That would be great, thanks
9. buy a cake
10. I like to bake

DAY 42 Other Plans

MATCHING

1. c   2. a   3. d   4. e   5. b

CONVERSATION

1. Would you like a drink
2. Did you hear about
3. I can't make it
4. That's too bad
5. out of town
6. Don't worry about it
7. wish her happy birthday
8. should get together
9. Good luck with your trip
10. Don't mention it

DAY 43 Party Preparation

MATCHING

1. e   2. a   3. c   4. b   5. d

CONVERSATION

1. Did you bring
2. some balloons and a birthday banner
3. When is Kim coming
4. in the kitchen
5. What kind of snacks
6. mixed nuts, crackers, and cheese
7. from the ceiling
8. This looks great
9. Could you help me with this banner

DAY 44 Wrapping a Gift

MATCHING

1. b   2. d   3. c   4. e   5. a

CONVERSATION

1. What's next
2. got her a vase for flowers
3. Where did you get it
4. if I may ask   5. I got it for $25
6. That's really cheap   7. are on sale
8. I'll go check it out   9. We're done

DAY 45 At the Party

MATCHING

1. b   2. d   3. a   4. e   5. c

CONVERSATION

1. Thanks for coming
2. I wouldn't miss it
3. put this gift
4. I'll take that
5. I'm glad you could come
6. make the cake   7. looks delicious
8. Let's sing   9. make a wish
10. Who is this from   11. I'm glad you like it

DAY 46 Getting a Haircut

MATCHING

1. d   2. b   3. a   4. e   5. c

CONVERSATION

1. How can I help you
2. need a haircut
3. have a seat
4. How would you like
5. Do you live in
6. Could you trim my sideburns
7. Do you want me to wash your hair
8. How much do I owe you
9. You can keep the change

DAY 47 Lost and Found

MATCHING

1. c   2. d   3. e   4. b   5. a

CONVERSATION

1. I think I left my bag here
2. No, I'm afraid not
3. a green sports bag
4. What brand is it
5. How big is it
6. It's nylon with canvas straps
7. What was in it
8. Can I have your name
9. if it turns up

DAY 48 A Cooking Lesson

MATCHING

1. d   2. a   3. c   4. b   5. e

CONVERSATION

1. What are we making
2. my grandmother's recipe
3. What should I do
4. How much cheese
5. Please chop up these onions and peppers
6. fry them in butter
7. Is this OK
8. They look perfect
9. That smells great
10. We have plenty, so please help yourself to more

DAY 49 The Date

MATCHING

1. b   2. a   3. d   4. c   5. e

CONVERSATION

1. I had a date with a guy named Mark
2. How did it go
3. I had a great time
4. What did you do
5. took me out to dinner
6. went to the Italian restaurant
7. The food was wonderful and the restaurant was very romantic
8. What does he look like
9. He has dark hair and a great smile
10. What is he like
11. great sense of humor
12. you guys really hit it off
13. We're going out again this weekend

DAY 50 A Movie Discussion

MATCHING

1. e   2. b   3. c   4. d   5. a

CONVERSATION

1. What are you doing this weekend
2. are going to see a movie
3. Oh, Julia and I saw that
4. What did you think
5. I don't like romantic movies very much
6. What kind of movies do you like
7. I really like thrillers
8. I like sci-fi movies
9. How did you like the special effects
10. I thought the acting was good, too
11. Who is your favorite actor
12. And he can play many roles, too